Most modern people go through life without reflecting on God's presence in the world around us. If God exists, then he is a long way off and not too concerned with our boring lives. But into this modern mindset, which is functionally atheistic, Benton Hall writes true tales of his journey with God in the everyday. At the golf course and at the dinner table, on the open road and on the bike path God is with us.

THE REV. CANON DAVID ROSEBERRY
Rector of Christ Church, Provincial Canon for Mission

Benton Hall is a hero to me. He has faithfully followed his calling to love and disciple young lives--and he has done it for years. His stories and insights arise from real life and will encourage all who take the time to read. I'm glad he is making this book available to us.

DUDLEY HALL
President of Kerygma Ventures and author of Grace Works

My uncle Benton has always been able to tie his life's personal journey into the bigger picture for others to follow. He has acted as a spiritual mentor for me as a youngster, throughout my years in the military, and during college at Texas. He took me boating down the Rogue River as a boy, officiated both my siblings' weddings (and will likely do mine one day). Benton is well known in our family as a fun husband, father, son, and brother, always providing us with truth, inspiration, and a special touch of his Uncle Benny humor of course...

NATE BOYER
Former Special Forces, U.Texas and Seattle Seahawks Deep Snapper

Tales from the Bike Path

Benton Hall

Clovercroft Publishing

Tales from the Bike Path

©2016 by Benton Hall

Published by Clovercroft Publishing, Franklin, Tennessee

Published in association with Larry Carpenter of Christian Book Services, LLC of Franklin, Tennessee

Edited by Gail Fallen

Cover Design by Matt Larseingue

Interior Layout Design by Suzanne Lawing

ISBN: 978-1-942557-20-3

Printed in the United States of America

Sunset, Sunrise

Texas sunsets and sunrises paint the skies across the great northern view from the backyard of my home in Plano, Texas. The backyard rolls out onto a bike path. My wife, Susie, and I appreciate the sense of open space. This great grassy area stretches for miles east and west, ribboned down the center with a concrete bike path; or should we say a "people path"? For people of all sizes, determinations, degrees of friendliness, and purpose drift and glide along past our home. Coyote have loped along the pathway at night. Skunks on the path acknowledged our Brittany Spaniel's "on point" stance one evening, sending a cascade of fragrance wafting his way. He never flinched! We did.

This path has provided much amusement for us and facilitated many relationships. We have made friends with the regulars on the path. It's been a quick twenty-four years since we moved onto the path. All three children have grown up, finished college, and established themselves in other cities. As kids they played soccer and baseball back there, hit golf balls, and rode bikes to school on the path. The working title for this tome became *Tales from the Bike Path*, for so much of our life has played out there, and a large chunk of the book has been scripted from our back patio overlooking the path.

Each of these stories reflect an aspect of God's heart, as he has revealed himself in situations from both work and life. There are numerous studies on the names of God and his attributes. An examination of all of them would be way beyond the purposes of this quick read. So each story title was crafted to point to an aspect of God's heart or his ways. It's my hope you will know him better through each story and ultimately enjoy and trust him more.

Purpose for the Tales

Growing up in Ft. Worth, my brothers Randy, Phil, and I regularly hiked into a world of adventure on Edwards Ranch, just over the ridge behind our home. We would disappear into the woods, pellet guns tucked under our arms and pockets full of sandwiches, exploring, climbing trees, making forts, shooting birds, or floating down the Trinity River. It was thrilling knowing we were free to roam on our adventures. Days exploring this ranch mirror my current life of adventure following Christ. My hope is that as you peruse these stories, you will be encouraged to develop an adventurous life of faith and grace by saying yes to the Lord's leading in your life.

After some academically unfruitful and morally foggy years of college, I was bushwhacked by God in Southern California. About the time I garnered my business degree from Texas, the US economy went into the dipper. *Time* magazine ran a story highlighting Harvard grads who painted houses for a living. Without any real job opportunities on the horizon, I pitched in with some guys from a different fraternity to sell books door to door with the Southwestern Company. Instead of going home after graduation, I headed for California. Within days, I noticed something different about these guys. They had been discipled by Cru, formerly Campus Crusade for Christ, a worldwide movement of evangelism and discipleship, headquartered in Orlando, Florida. They were enjoying devotions each morning before work and invited me to join them.

It took a couple of weeks of studying David Reed, my boarding house roommate, to convince me. David had been a high school quarterback and was the grandson of a well-known Dallas retailer. He was real, he was fun, and he was serious about his faith. Casting stubborn resistance aside, I joined the group one morning in San Diego's Balboa Park. After I shared my story of receiving God's forgiveness at Episcopal Camp Crucis, they began to fill in the blank spaces of what I knew about God. It took days, as there were lots of blank spaces. They were studying Miles Stanford's *The Green Letters,* the section on God's unconditional love.

I grabbed onto the truth that God loved me like a drowning man going down for the final time. On my sales routes for the next month, I would repeatedly tell myself, "He loves me unconditionally right now, no matter what I am doing." My self-image began to be restored on his truth, not based on my accomplishments. Returning to Ft. Worth, I got involved in a Cru adult study, which met next door to my folks. After a year and a half of discipleship with Jim Slaughter in this group, volunteering at TCU with Cru, and leading high school small groups with my brother Randy, I joined Cru full time in the fall of 1972. When I discovered they had an outreach to high schools, I knew instinctively this was God's way for me.

Forty-three years later, here I sit planted on the former cotton fields of Plano, Texas. Having survived prior stints in Colorado and Minnesota, I am literally blocks away from the location of one of my best dove hunting days ever back in '74. On a break from work in Boulder, Colorado, I had joined TCU amigo Guy Owen at the Dallas Seminary for his classes in the morning. We dove hunted in the afternoon near what is now a Verizon transfer station, at Marchman and Legacy Drive. Collin County has historically been great dove hunting country, and I am now searching out ripe and ready souls in those same fields! In the next stories, you will hear how the Lord has worked in our Cru ministry and a little more of my personal story. It's my prayer that you be encouraged, amused, and uplifted. He is an awesome God who resides far beyond the circumstances of our lives and yet also somehow right in the middle of them at the same time, always wooing us to trust him and fall back onto his unconditional love.

Tennis Ball Guerrilla Warfare – A Night of Justice and Mercy

One of the greatest adventures in my life, alongside a thirty-eight year marriage and raising three kids, is working with high school students. A recent story from the bike path happened this spring, when I hosted the high school guys for an evening Bible study. Thirty of us went out into the darkness along the bike path to play "Tennis Ball Guerrilla Warfare." It's an adapted game of Capture the Flag that friend Steve Cooper and I concocted where players fire tennis balls at each other instead of tagging by hand. It seems to be more fun in the dark. After twenty minutes of running and yelling on the path, with tennis balls flying in every direction, one of my neighbors stepped out in his pajamas with a shotgun to loudly inquire what was going on! The panting, wide-eyed student reporting this episode excitedly assured me he had never experienced anything like this in his home city, New Orleans.

A short time later, another nervous neighbor called Plano's finest. A squad car rolled up the bike path and an officer's spot lighted four of the guys. Three of them turned to the fourth guy and in unison yelled, "Run, Henry, run!" While Henry sprinted away, Michael Wang, one of our Cru student leaders, responsibly approached the officer and explained what was going on. When he learned the game was part of a Bible study, the officer nodded, rolled up his window, and, mercifully, slowly cruised away without comment. Desiring to inflict no further consternation upon my good neighbors, we shut down the game and reconvened the sweaty group inside for our lesson. Without fun games like these and pizza, there would not be much ministry to high school boys. That night goes down in the annals of history as just another unforgettable evening on the bike path! Perhaps justice wasn't enforced on behalf of some of the neighbors, but God mercifully intervened with a policeman who understood boys and appreciated any efforts to teach them from the Bible!

Six Crows and a Hawk –
A Scene of Omnipotence

A loud racket broke out on the easement one morning the day after a conversation with some football players. Six crows' loud cawing drew me out past our red oak to catch a view of the ornithological drama. A red-tailed hawk sat perched high atop the utility pole, peacefully minding his business. As he scoped the path for any quick movements of breakfast morsels, the crows cawed loudly, trying to shove him out of their perceived area. They had surrounded him at safe distances to protest loudly.

In that moment, I sensed this "hawk vs. crow" scenario was reflective of my visit with the athletes the day before. I was cast in the role of the hawk, and the crows represented all the distractions . . . harmlessly cawing like these crows.

It had been a crazy day that gracefully ended with several

boys trusting in Christ. While visiting with these guys after practice, we had several major distractions: loud mowers, the girls drill team, etc., but the guys took it all in stride and stayed focused all the way through to the closing prayer.

A friend had seen this "hawk vs. crow" drama play out in another state. That hawk finally had enough and turned quickly in flight to attack one of the pesky crows chasing him. My friend said the crow disappeared in a poof! Disconnected pieces of taloned crow parts and feathers drifted slowly to Earth, proof of the hawk's winged superiority. Engaged in the Lord's work and filled with his Spirit, we too enjoy the same superiority in spiritual warfare. The clatter can seem loud, distracting, and even deafening at times, yet our God reigns supreme in warfare over the expansion of his kingdom. As the cross demonstrates, even when it appears we are losing, victory is being secured by our all- powerful God.

Jerry, the ATF, and NYC Firemen – A Time of Sacrifice

Directly across the bike path from us, several homes were built on vacant lots after we moved onto ours. My admiration for a porch cover on one of them set me up for a visit. Neighbor Jerry had been an ATF agent for years in Dallas. He was very friendly and we became bike path acquaintances.

A couple of years later, I noticed neighbor Jerry washing his cars over and over and over. It was just after the David Koresh standoff in Waco. I approached him during one of these strange endless washings . . .

"Jerry, what's going on? These cars can't be *that* dirty." He turned with huge tears in his eyes and said, "Benton, I trained most of those men [the ATF agents] who died in Waco and this is the only way I know how to handle it. I just keep washing my cars." Tears began to find pathways down my cheeks.

Responsible men, caring and grieving over other men. There is something good about this that runs deep. It's some of what God intended for men, I think: doing the hard things, sacrificial things. Like the NYC firemen who continued down those lower Manhattan streets toward the second tower after the first building had collapsed on 9/11. They knew, they *had* to know, they were rushing along to the cadence of their own death march. Men know and still they march, and I am honored to know some of these men. Oh, they love the adventure, the confirmation of manhood, the camaraderie, the mission . . . but they each embrace the death march at some level, and this march puts them into a spirituality that prayerfully links them to God.

The Right Stuff – A Season of Bravery and Partnership

My dad was awarded the Distinguished Flying Cross as a WWII fighter pilot. Dad served three years in the Army Air Corps. Like many in the late 1930s, Dad saw the war with Germany developing while in high school and picked up his pilot's license as a teen. After a couple of rough years in the Corps at Texas A&M, he escaped into the Army Air Corps. Because he was a good pilot, they wanted him to be a flight trainer in Corpus Christi. Desiring combat instead, Dad promptly went up and got purposely lost. Just lost enough to still get sent overseas to India, where he was part of the second wave of men to join the First Air Commandos. They flew sorties against the Japanese in the China-Burma-India Theater, commonly referred to as the CBI. His outfit was the first special operations unit ever assembled. The first group had

My Dad's P-47, "Straw Benny Jam"mechanics on the wing

been handpicked by John Allison and Philip Cochran to assist the British in retaking Burma. Dad flew the P-47 Thunderbolt and the famous P-51 Mustang . . . the fastest prop fighters in US history.

Dad says his faith was galvanized during wartime, and I have learned lessons from his experience. He said the cautious pilots inevitably got shot down and those who went full out seemed to survive. So, I want to go all out. It is on this front edge that I find God . . . or at least, his trail. J. R. R. Tolkien's hobbit Bilbo Baggins found more help on the way to adventure than he found by the warm hearth fire of his cozy den.

Dad was shot down by anti-aircraft fire over Burma, crash landing behind enemy lines around 3 p.m. Pilots carried 45s on them and he had a fold-up carbine strapped to the inside of his cockpit. When his plane rolled to a stop on the grass landing strip, he popped his canopy, ready to shoot it out. Off to his left, he noticed a British Pathe' News reporter coming out of the jungle just off the runway. He recognized him right away as British, with knee socks, khaki jacket, and pith helmet. The Brits had regained this hallowed ground earlier in the day at 10 a.m. In a brisk and clipped British accent, the newsman asked if my father would re-emerge from the cockpit because they wanted to capture it all on film! He gladly consented, and somewhere in the archives of British war footage, my Dad, a virile young lieutenant, is featured on celluloid, doing what men are called on to do each day . . . the brave thing. Your brave thing may be simply partnering with God for help to show up at a not-so-good work place on time each day. Whatever your brave thing, get hooked on the rush that comes from partnering by faith.

Surprised by God – A Season of Grace and Love

Grace has been an easy biblical concept for me to grab on to because my parents were gracious. One summer while in junior high, I snuck out my bedroom window past curfew to continue to play with my friends. I had bad asthma growing up and doctors thought the night air was harmful, so I had an earlier curfew than the rest of the neighborhood. I would peek out my window after being tucked in for the night and listen to the joyful sounds of all my neighborhood friends still up playing. Since I thrive on being with people, it killed me that they were out there and I wasn't! So a plan was hatched. I first stuffed my bed with clothes to make it look like I was in it. Out the window I bolted, soon having a blast with friends down the street. It was easy to sneak back in later, so the next night, off I went again.

When I arrived home the second night, my bedroom window had been locked and wouldn't budge. Dum, De, Dum, Dum! Panicked, I knew the only way back in was through the front door. Dad was working in the garage on something. I knew he saw me, but nothing was said. I was in deep trouble. Sneaking in and crawling into bed, I lay fearfully awake awaiting my fate. My treachery had been discovered when my nearsighted Mom had come in to kiss me goodnight and made contact with the pillows and clothes I had stuffed into bed. She screamed and my fate was sealed while I played joyfully unaware down the street.

Both parents came into my room after an eternity of sweating it out and praying little-boy prayers of repentance. As typical children growing up in the '50s and '60s, our behavior had been finely and consistently honed by the acceptable corporeal disciplines of the day, so what happened next surprised me. My folks told me they felt they had been overprotective and decided to extend my curfew. Unbelievable! How could a guy not learn about grace from parents like that?

My brothers and I served as altar boys . . . imagine Tom Sawyer robed in cassock, halo slightly askew. There were 7 a.m. Eucharists each morning requiring an altar boy, and we were usually scheduled in several times each month. It was in the quietness of those hours that I began to dig deep into the mysteries of God. There was a great painting in the back of the chapel of Jesus as a carpenter with his arms crossed above some woodwork, smiling at you. Whoa. Just stop right there. Jesus smiled? Yes, and his eyes followed you everywhere in that chapel! All seeing, all knowing, all powerful, and yet, he smiles. More grace. I noticed that on some days it was only Mom and me and Father Barnes at Mass. I asked what would happen if I was sick one of those days and couldn't make it. How could God and Father Barnes carry on without us?

Mom said the Lord would understand that I was sick, and that it would be OK. Father Barnes would conduct mass without us. That sunk in deep. I wasn't on a performance basis with this God. Grace upon grace; my life has dripped with the sweet aroma of it, and I am determined to pass it on. The guys in our movement regularly hear me say that God is crazy about them. I want to pound this truth into them. If they can begin to grasp his unconditional love, they become free of guilt and shame, step out of culturally reinforced self-absorption, and reach out to their friends. Grace is powerful and restorative, and I can't seem to experience enough!

Instruction from the Father –
A Matter of Omniscience

In April 2010, having been encouraged by *Final Rounds*, a father/son story of growing up in golf, I wanted to reconnect on the course. Dad still played, haunting the fairways and the dining halls of Colonial Country Club. As I joined him and brother Phil for lunch in the Club Room, we discussed the second coming, current events, and life. Out on the practice surface, we pulled over some teakwood chairs and got set up. Dad began softly directing and encouraging. Starting with the flop wedge, I swung away. The balls, scudding away in various directions at first, began to straighten their flights. The handle of a driver was laid lightly on my head as Dad worked to eliminate all unnecessary movement. I swung, rotating around my right leg, with an open stance and wrists locked. The shots began to cluster beautifully around a flag some distance away.

OK sports fans, it's not a far drift from taking golf instructions from my father to taking direction from my heavenly Father. The joy of the fellowship is amplified and the direction is tailor-made just for us. Its direction lovingly crafted by the Master Craftsman and empowered by his Holy Spirit. In his omniscience, he knows how we operate best and what he has planned for us.

Just before my dad quit playing at Colonial, I brought two of my coach buddies over for a round. Stephen Hardy and Matt Sipes had always wanted to play the famous Ft. Worth course. I had warned them about what a tease my dad was, so they were ready and excited. It was an entirely wonderful day with Dad. The four of us had a blast, and it was a joy to share him with my friends for a day. This joyful fellowship was enhanced by our love for Christ and the acknowledgement of his presence. Even in our recreation, he continues to delight in us, and there are lessons to be learned in every aspect of our lives. As we bring all things into subjection under the power of the Spirit, our lives become conformed to the image of Christ and reflect him at work and at play.

The God who Nudges –
A Moment of Partnership
in His Purposes

While running errands in my Lexus SUV, I got the nudge from the Lord to call a mom of two guys in our movement. Friends Doug and Holly Brooks had graciously donated the SUV to our work. I had given the mom our previous SUV, also donated, and was checking on whether her son could join us at our camp in Colorado. Friends had provided a scholarship for him. As we spoke I sensed a heaviness in her speech, and without much prodding, some real concerns began to spill out. Asking if I could pray for her over the phone, the Spirit seemed to give me words; protection from the Devil and for a closer walk with him. She was so grateful, saying she really needed that.

How does all that work? There I am riding high in a nice SUV and another child in the Lord is suffering. The Lord works through this dissonance every day. All situations are different at different times, yet God is the same, immutable, shepherding each, crying with some, rejoicing with some, loving all.

You Were Born for This by Bruce Wilkinson was pushed on me by friend and pastor Lloyd Spence. It's a book about nudges from the Lord. Nudges are those moments when you are convinced the Lord is leading you to say or do something. Anyone who has walked in faith for a while can confirm their existence. It's fun to join up with the Lord on his missions, long-term and short-term. Some require lots of preparation, some are short, and all are usually scary and require faith steps.

While working in Boulder, one of the staff and longtime friends, Vic Waters, had made a trip home to raise needed financial support. After a couple weeks, he called on the way to his home airport, saying he was flying to Colorado to pack up and leave staff, moving home to teach and coach. Like having phones in both ears, I was surprised to hear the Lord's nudge . . . "Tell him he's not leaving staff and you will raise the rest of his support."

Not being the world's best fundraiser, and not wanting to upset Vic's parents, I fought myself for a millisecond till I heard a familiar and forceful voice say, "No, you're not leaving staff! You go back home and pack up for Boulder. I will raise your funds!" Vic told me his mom would be angry at me, which I said would be fine; blame it all on me. We hung up and I wondered, "What was that, Lord?"

Vic returned to Boulder, and amazingly, it seemed, we raised up all the needed funds locally. He continued to crank out a great student ministry at Boulder High and later in Minneapolis. After attending Bethel Seminary, Vic now pastors in Minnesota.

Don't be afraid to join the Lord in these adventures of faith. He is standing in the deep water, asking you to jump and trust that he will catch you.

Waiting on God during Hurry-Up Days – A Time of His Provision

After six years and three kids, we outgrew our first home in Plano and began trying to sell it. After four years of failed attempts, a Realtor arrived one day with two sisters from Thailand. Stepping into our home's entryway, they noticed brass art objects from Thailand that missionary friends had given us. The sisters became convinced we knew their country. It seems they loved things about our house we didn't: the small yard they could mow quickly and the busy intersection near-by, allowing them to quickly come and go to their two jobs. Returning in the late evenings, they weren't bothered by day-time traffic that had become so loud in the last several years. The Realtor shook her head in disbelief as she told us she had shown them a hundred homes just like our Fox and Jacobs, but they liked ours.

So God was working! Immediately we had to make a mad dash for a rental home in August just before school started. Having been told several times that the listed home I was calling about was already rented, I sensed the need to step up my game. I usually don't sense the Lord leading me into a rush, but this was a time for quick, decisive action. I found a home listing similar in size to ours and at the right price. The agent said he had a showing at 7 p.m. that night. Fine, I told him, I would crash that party at 6 p.m. with a cash deposit. We lived in that rental for six months while I prayed, "Lord, what do we do now? Buy a used home, a new home, build a home, or rent?"

One morning, in the quietness of the early hour, I sensed him nudge me, saying, "We will do whatever you want to trust me for." Rats! I wanted him to pick the house, but I knew this was a test of my faith, and as I talked it over with Susie, we decided to trust him to build what has become our current home.

Former students and Cru staff from Plano, Lee and Stephanie Cooksey, told us about some home builders from Stephanie's church, Don and Beverly Linebarger. We liked this humble and honest couple from our first meeting. Don would work the building site while Beverly lined up subcontractors and took bids. They could build us a home that would fit our needs, just like a couple of others they had built previously in the same neighborhood. They already had one particular lot in mind. It had been frozen off the market during the savings and loan crisis of the late '80s and was just a mile away from our first home. It was the first lot in that neighborhood to come available.

Beverly called the S&L that owned the land, and they told

her to fax a bid. She had never faxed anything. Driving home that day, she passed a sign in a printer's window that said FAX. She sensed the Lord wanted her to stop right then and fax a bid. She turned the car around and went in. They showed her how the fax worked, and our bid sailed off across the wires. An hour later another bid came in on top of ours. Ours was first, so we got this special lot. Thanks, Beverly, for listening to the Lord!

It's been a great neighborhood to raise kids and a key neighborhood in our ministry to students. We can see the Lord's fingerprints all over this move. There are some decisions in life that have larger financial consequences and require more time before the eternal Lord. We don't seem to enjoy the waiting as much as he does. His throne sits above time and space, so waiting is no big deal for him. The psalmist describes the benefits of waiting in Psalms 130:1–8, "A Song of Ascents" (English Standard Version):

My Soul Waits for the Lord

Out of the depths I cry to you, O Lord!

O Lord, hear my voice! Let your ears be attentive to the voice of my pleas for mercy!

If you, O Lord, should mark iniquities, O Lord, who could stand?

But with you there is forgiveness, that you may be feared.

I wait for the Lord, my soul waits, and in his word I hope;

my soul waits for the Lord more than watchmen for the morning,

more than watchmen for the morning.

> *O Israel, hope in the Lord! For with the Lord there is steadfast love,*
>
> *and with him is plentiful redemption.*
>
> *And he will redeem Israel from all his iniquities.*

So all his best to you who wait, patiently or under duress. I know how you feel and I know how your waiting ends . . . with you pressed deeper in the knowledge of how he works, who he is, and how much he loves you.

An Errant Golf Ball – A Glimpse of God's Love

Hitting golf balls into the neighbor's backyards is a recreational hazard, especially when you swing like me and live on the bike path. Our daughter, Heather, while a member of the Plano Sr. High golf team, sliced a practice ball into our neighbor's back yard or through his window; we were not quite sure which. In training children, I find it good to address these situations as quickly as possible. We immediately marched across the golf course (the utility easement) to the out-of-bounds area (the neighbor's home) and knocked on the door. My Malaysian neighbor answered; his name was Koh. I explained that our errant ball was somewhere in his backyard bunker and had possibly broken something. He didn't seem to hear any of this because he was so encouraged that a neighbor had engaged him in conversation. He insisted we come inside

. . . after we first removed our shoes.

Within minutes, Koh was telling me his life story as we searched the backyard for the ball. Realizing the Lord may have directed this errant nine-iron shot into a strategic bunker, I told him about our work with students. All this was totally foreign to Koh, who was raised agnostic. Anyway, we became friends that day.

Koh grew up in the countryside of Malaysia near lakes, swollen rice paddies full of tropical fish, and picturesque mountains. Enjoying a great outdoor lifestyle as a child, he was hoping to recapture some of this adventure when he bought a small fishing boat without his wife's knowledge. We had some adventures on this fine craft . . . like leaving the dock without putting the plug in . . . taking on enormous amounts of water and barely retreating to safety before capsizing.

Koh was so ashamed, but I think my humble and almost uncontrollable laughter helped him reclaim his dignity. On our maiden voyage, Murphy's Law basically held court. If anything could go wrong, it *did*! I have pictures from that trip of a couple guys out on a lake fishing, but I have no pictures of anyone actually catching anything. There were subsequent trips which produced the same non-bountiful harvest of freshwater fish and more opportunities to share the gospel and explore Koh's beliefs.

Over time I discovered how much the Lord had been at work on Koh. At a birthday party for his son, I learned some of his coworkers had been witnessing to him at work. God had also positioned the strong Christian parents of one of our student leaders as his supervisors. It's amazing the lengths the Lord goes to behind the scenes to express his love. Don't give up praying for friends or family. Assume the Lord is at work, as he is with Koh. I saw the Lord reel in a good friend after thirty-five years of prayer. I assume if the Lord puts someone across my path in some significant way, it's for a purpose. He loves them far more than I, and with that, I begin to engage in joyful and patient anticipation of what God is working in their lives! Sometimes I get to see the fruition of prayers, sometimes I don't. It's my job to pray as he remains faithful.

The Power of Discretion – A Time of Omniscience

One week after securing my driver's license at the age of fifteen, I accidentally hit a boy on a bicycle in my neighborhood. He survived with a chipped tooth and scratched elbow, and seven years later attended some of my first Bible studies. The ambulance and his folks arrived within minutes, whisking him away. I was left alone curbside for the next forty-five minutes. My mom's red Nash Rambler station wagon sat skidded sideways in the middle of the street, a boy's bike protruding out from under the front bumper. You cannot imagine the accusing glares I garnered that day as I sat waiting for the police. The same police, who, upon measuring my skid marks, determined I was not speeding, thank you!

My dad paid all the hospital expenses, and that was the wrap on this scary incident of my youth, or so I thought. Years later as an adult, I learned the boy's family had waited twelve months till the statute of limitations was about to expire to sue my folks and win a sizable amount of money.

I never heard any of this from my father. And as I think of it, I can't recall my father ever impugning anyone personally, apart from dispersions regularly cast toward the play of the Dallas Cowboys. Important things run in families from fathers to sons like truthfulness and honor.

My father served on the leadership board of an organization when the head guy was found to have acted in such a way that dismissal was necessary. The board deemed the offense serious enough for termination, but decided against public disgrace. They backed this good man as he secured other employment. We do serve a God of second chances, a merciful God who does change our lives, and they believed God would reconcile this man's career. They maintained silence over the cause of his dismissal, choosing not to besmirch his character, so they did not inform the members of the organization of his specific indiscretion. And for that they took some heat. The leader was well liked.

But they believed that before God, they were to remain silent, and so they did. It was a sacrificial discretion well purposed and well done before a sovereign God, without regard for personal or public justification. The Spirit causes us to look to ourselves lest we also sin. Realizing it could have easily been my own falling which required discretion, I am grateful for his grace . . . an awesome grace which causes us to tremble, tremble, tremble.

As we walk in the power of the Spirit, trusting him with the details of life, we reflect our heavenly Father's character: his love, joy, and patience . . . and hopefully some discretion. We can trust this omniscient, all-knowing God that not every story needs an airing. He knows and we can rest in that.

In the Midst of Tragedy –
A Season of Faithfulness

Evangelism is at the core of the Father's heart and a large part of what we do in Cru. Under Chuck Klein's leadership, we ran summer projects in Estes Park with high school students for several years in the seventies. We lived in apartments and houses, helped students secure jobs at restaurants and hotels; discipled them on weekends and evenings. One week we planned an elaborate outreach, with creative evangelism all over the city. We also committed prayer time to back it up and it was stewarded by my friend, Zeke, Donald Zeiler who headed up our Houston movement.

One of the more creative things we did was set up a booth like Lucy used in the *Peanuts* comic strip to disperse advice for a nickel, complete with a colorful banner across the top asking, "Why are you in the mountains?" Our booth was placed at the mouth of an alley, just off the main sidewalk downtown next to a bar called The Wheel, pictured below. Students and staff manned the booth all week, taking surveys about why people came to the mountains, then transitioning to the gospel. Many days, the alley would fill up with people in small groups hearing the Good News about the Mountain Maker. Many locals and tourists made decisions to accept God's love and forgiveness that week, not only at the booth but also all over the city. Most of the action, however, was at the booth on Main Street, next to the bar.

The owner of The Wheel got nervous mid-week and complained about the booth. Amidst much prayer and petition, we assured him we would be finished by the end of the week and he agreed to let us continue. I think we had some sort of permit and permission from the city. This was our only opposition, as best I can recall, till Saturday evening . . . when it began to rain.

The Big Thompson Flood

Our team of staff and students had prayed asking the Lord to hold back the Evil One that week in particular. The last day of our week of evangelism activities, Saturday night, produced an increasingly heavy rain. By midevening, we had wrapped up the week's events and headed for the sack, rejoicing in all the Lord had accomplished. Just as we were turning in, a tremendous lightning storm developed around Estes. The guys in my house all crowded around a big picture window to watch until it struck so close and so powerfully, we all retreated to the middle of the room. Zeke Zeiler reported seeing lightning dance down the mountains toward his cabin through his bathroom window. It was a unique end to our week.

Around 11 p.m. or so, my Estes neighbor came over all excited and wanted me to drive around with him in his old International Scout and check out the flooding. He had heard things on a police scanner, I think. We piled into his Scout, and I recall driving through an empty downtown and seeing the water beginning to rise over the curbs. I wasn't too concerned, as these types of rain are common in Texas. We drove out east of town on Highway 36 onto the Crocker Ranch. My neighbor's friend managed it for Sun Oil. We couldn't find any signs of flooding, so we returned home.

The next morning at church, we got reports of flooding down the Big Thompson Canyon along Highway 34. Sadly, the number of deaths due to the flood was growing.

Our annual all-staff training had begun in Ft. Collins at CSU, and half of us had planned to drive down for the day. We got word the Big Thompson Canyon was blocked, so we drove around through Lyons. Upon reaching the CSU campus, people came running over to our cars asking us if we knew about the flood. Still puzzled, we learned that several Cru staff women were unaccounted for, including Dr. Bright's wife, Vonette. They had been on a women's retreat near the mouth of the canyon at Sylvan Dale Ranch. Later, several of the women hiked out of the area, including Vonette. Nine of the women had passed away when their two cars were swept off bridges by the rising water and carried downstream. Only two of the women from these cars lived to tell the story.

Later, I returned to the Crocker Ranch to discover that had we driven one hundred yards farther that night into the ranch, we would have encountered a huge mud and dirt slide across the property. Some of our staff women, including my future wife, had considered driving down to Ft. Collins from Estes the evening of the flooding to spend the night at CSU. They could have easily been caught up in the high waters. One hundred and forty-four people died that night.

Cru staff had to go to the makeshift morgue in Loveland to identify the nine staff women. They were amazed at their peaceful faces compared to horrified looks on others in the morgue. The two girls who escaped the cars (and floated away to be picked up later) reported that an incredible peace had come over the vehicles as the water rose in them. I am not guaranteeing a painless transition into eternity for anyone, but once on the other side, we have guarantees upon guarantees from our faithful Lord himself, and on these I put my faith.

"Let not your hearts be troubled. Believe in God; believe also in me. In my Father's house are many rooms. If it were not so, would I have told you that I go to prepare a place for you? And if I go and prepare a place for you, I will come again and will take you to myself, that where I am you may be also."
— JOHN 14:1–3 ESV

While We Play –
A Time of Patience

For almost eleven years, my day couldn't start without Hunter, our Brittany Spaniel. I learned many a life lesson with Hunter. Most mornings we followed a semi-normal routine of drifting out into the front yard early enough so that we wouldn't disturb or scare any of the neighborhood walkers. Comfortably seated under our live oak on a concrete bench, I drank hot coffee while trying to remember my name and saying good morning to God. Hunter roamed the empty neighborhood, sniffing out rabbits, squirrels, and traces of his canine brothers who had loped down the sidewalks with masters in tow the night before.

Hunter made wide sweeping forays out to my right and then, after some time, darted past me and swept off to my left. This is the natural hunting instinct of the Brittany. Afterwards we would retreat inside for my concentrated time with the Lord. One morning Hunter grabbed one of his plastic colored balls and began growling and rolling around with it somewhere in my vicinity as I knelt beside the couch. He thinks the ball has some life of its own as it rolls away from his punching, prying paws and disappears under the couch. I retrieve these errant toys and roll them out, where they are again pounced upon with much glee.

This morning it seems like I am under the couch four or five times, fetching the ball (who is training whom here?). Becoming slightly annoyed by the interruptions to my time with the Lord, I began to ponder. Does God treat me like I treat Hunter? Does he clean up my messes, while sovereignly lavishing his grace? Does he patiently roll out my ball again and again? What kind of God is this that enjoys my bumbling fellowship, kicking around the base of his throne? It's the same loving Father whose Son "died for all, that those who live might no longer live for themselves but for him who for their sake died and was raised" (2 Cor. 5:15).

Coffee, Tea, and Persian Friends – A Season of Purpose

Starbucks built a store in my neighborhood. We have conducted numerous appointments, Bible studies, and staff meetings here, and it continues to generate new and interesting stories. There had been a group of Middle Eastern men who began to gather there each evening around dinnertime. I really wanted to join this group. My friendship with Middle Easterners goes back to 1975 when I worked in Estes Park for the summer. A Persian national team soccer player named Jilal backed into my Camaro one afternoon and insisted we become friends, which we did. Years later Zee Askari moved in next door to us, and we became friends.

Months after Zee had moved and begun renting out his home, I caught his tenants sneaking away in the middle of the night. Alerting Zee, I made him promise to call the police before he came. They arrived together. Zee read these guys the riot act. I listened from my dining room window as he recited how proud he was to become a US citizen and asked accusingly, "How could they do this thing, skipping out on the rent, in such a great and God-fearing country?" I was moved to put my hand over my heart. As he spoke, the policeman slipped silently behind the men and began handcuffing them on outstanding warrants. Honestly, I was and am so proud to know Zee.

So I was praying to meet these Middle Eastern guys at my Starbucks. One afternoon I pulled in when I noticed a couple of them drinking hot tea outside while my car thermometer read 103 degrees. Stepping out of the car, I inquired, smiling, "How can you do this?" And Shon replied, "It's Persian tea!" Bells went off in my heart as I asked, "Are you guys Persians?!"

These men grafted me into their fellowship. We began visiting regularly and drinking hot tea. I learned about the Middle East from a new perspective while sailing around in my gospel ship, looking for a port where I could dock. That day was my first of many glasses of Persian tea. They instructed me to tuck a sugar cube between my gum and back tooth to sweeten the tea as it flowed over the tongue. These guys have helped me with car windshields, fig trees, and home air conditioning. The city passed a new ordinance about smoking near dining places, and the group of Persians has dispersed. We had many discussions about the grace of the gospel contrasted with the universalism of their Bahai faith. Historically, Persia was Zoroastrian until Islam was forced upon them in the seventh century. Members of the Bahai have been persecuted within Iran. Several of these guys had been conscripted to fight during the war with Iraq. One of them had been gassed. Another still had a bullet lodged in his leg. They had migrated to Pakistan and sought asylum in the US Embassy. They all loved their country but were so happy be in the United States.

Honey in the Coffee

Another evening at Starbucks, while putting milk in my Americano, I noticed a Persian-looking guy putting honey into his coffee. I made some fun banter about this oddity, and he encouraged me to try it. We smiled and I began to head out when the Lord administered a real and almost physical nudge. Immediately spinning around, I returned to visit with Masoud . . . asking him if he might be Persian. Fifteen minutes later, he is staring at me with this funny look, saying, "Benton, I have never talked to anyone like this; I have just told you my entire life." Maybe I am developing a knack for recognizing Persians and nudges.

We started a friendship that day. He had moved to Texas so his daughters could go to pharmacy school. He had invested in a cellular supply company down the sidewalk from my Starbucks. Some months later, he noticed me conducting a Bible study with a handful of guys in Starbucks during finals week. He was impressed that guys would study the Bible during finals. He didn't realize that boys would rather do anything than study during finals! As I introduced him, he was being friendly and trying to encourage everyone when he said something about all religions being the same.

I took a risk; I wagged my finger at him, and smilingly explained, "No, Masoud! Only Jesus died on the cross and came back to life, and no other religion invites you into a relationship with God!"

He was taken aback and, after some silence, said, "Benton, I'm leaving for two months to Iran. When I return we must sit down and you must teach me about these things!" Well, several months later, we talked about Jesus for almost an hour. I left him a DVD of the Jesus film in multiple languages, including his.

Scantron Christmas

In the fall, Masoud called needing my help with his appeal to a local university on behalf of his daughter, who was accused of cheating in a biology class. Because of the appeal, she was allowed to finish the class and achieved an A, but it was not credited. We spent hours pounding out the verbiage and strategy of her appeal. At one point Masoud got the president of the Scantron Company to admit that his machines made mistakes. This was a point crucial to his daughter's defense. He wanted me to go into business with him and we would sue the company. Yikes! I persuaded him that God would not honor us for suing them and that I couldn't work for anyone but Cru. But I wonder what a partnership we would have made!

One afternoon just before Christmas, we were working at his home. As we finished, I noticed there were no decorations. Asking if they knew that Persians were in attendance at the first Christmas, I shared the story of the Wise Men and the birth of Christ. They seemed interested. Days later, I called to check on the progress of the appeal. Masoud was laughing as he said, "Benton, my entire family is changed!" His daughters were imitating my laugh and had told their mom all about me. Three trips to the store later, Christmas lights were strung all over his house.

The university sided with the professor in the appeal, but they chose to release him the next fall. God mercifully intervened, and because she had appealed she was allowed to take biology over and made an A. Upon graduation, she entered pharmacy school in Arizona. Masoud has followed her there, and we still text occasionally. Don't you love the way the Lord prepares these relationships for you to step into? Just taking a tiny faith step can open up a whole new realm . . . a realm where I am learning that fig branches make the best skewers for shish kabob and that green unripened figs are great meat tenderizers. These are the kinds of things you can learn from a three-thousand-year-old culture!

Permission to Convert

In our work with students, we certainly have changed some lives on this front. Our athletic chapel meetings after practice are optional, and it's fun when Jewish or Muslim kids stick around for a cold drink with friends to hear our stories. Over the months and years, we've developed some good friendships, and I think the guys can sense how much I care about them and, therefore, how much the Lord cares about them. Several Persians have trusted Christ with us and some Jews have found their Messiah. One Persian student came to me at school one day and announced that his father had given him permission to convert to Christianity. His sister was a Christian and his father said he could be one too. Another student said he loved me and loved the chapels, but that his father would kill him if he converted. I stared at him for a moment silently inquiring, and he nodded his head yes as if to confirm my greatest fears. I'm still not sure what he meant, but I am certain it wouldn't have been pleasant. I assured him God was for him.

I don't like the conversion word. When someone trusts Christ, they become a new person and are adopted into his family with the rights and privileges of true children. If they have to wear the trappings of their family's historic religion for a while, God can deal with that. It also allows them an inside track to talk about Isa Al-Masih (Jesus Messiah) within their community. Most Muslims don't have a problem with Isa. He is featured prominently and positively in their book with more coverage than Mohammed.

One Muslim student came to some of our Bible studies when they were held in homes of friends. He had grown up with Christian friends who took him to church and loved on him. During his senior year, he trusted Christ. I called him one day during school thinking I could leave him an encouraging message. He surprised me by picking up. He explained that his teachers wouldn't believe he had converted and wanted to put me on the phone to convince them. Laughing, I told him that I would do no better explaining than he, and to quit using the term "converted"!

Into the Frozen North – A Year of Reluctant Partnership

After our first year of marriage spent working in Boulder, Susie and I accepted an assignment in Minneapolis, Minnesota. We enjoyed an incredible Indian summer, where fall seems to last forever. Beautiful colors were the norm in Hiawatha Park and all over the city. Then, December 1, winter descended upon us wrathfully and didn't let up till late April. It was the worst winter in recorded Minnesota history: fifty-seven days in a row of below freezing temps—mostly in the twenties—tons of snow, frozen pipes, frozen cars, and frozen people. Our previous assignment, Boulder, Colorado, seemed like a tropical paradise in comparison.

The night we moved into our apartment, I stayed up till 1 a.m. killing 101 mosquitos who had invited themselves to the feast. You know the mosquito, the state bird of North Dakota?

This is the kind of humor Minnesotans resort to in order to maintain sanity during the long winters.

One morning we had to use a hair dryer on the water pipes along the windows to thaw them out so we could have heat. Why they were there, I don't know, because even Texas builders know better than to leave water pipes along exterior walls! We had to rustproof our car, rent a garage, and stock the car with blankets, candles, and jumper cables in case we, or anyone else in Minnesota, got stranded in a blizzard somewhere. Hey, this is nothing to the Norse and Swedes: they live with this reality. I tip my Stetson to them; they truly are some hardy stock.

What a chapter, what memories. The Lord used us to help a ton of kids find faith, opening a door with the previously 1-10 football team. That season, as Steve Cooper and I worked with them, they marched three games deep into the playoffs and beat cross-town rivals Anoka in the Pumpkin Bowl on Halloween. We were on the sidelines, in practices, doing chapels, Bible studies, and early morning breakfasts, sharing the gospel.

Despite the weather, it was an awesome year of ministry. And one of my most memorable sporting events ever was the dual wrestling match with Anoka. Bobby Davis wrestled at 133 pounds and was growing in his faith. His coach, Bob Board, was one of the all-time great guys. (Susie and I hunkered down with their family in the basement of Bob's house later that spring during a tornado alert.) The match was a sellout. I found myself near the top of the bleachers; the gym was packed. There were some really good matchups that night, and Bobby was facing the state champ.

Cross Town Rivalry –
A Night of Faithfulness

As they took the mat, the crowd noise ratcheted up, and the ref gave the signal, standing between them lowering his arm and raising it quickly, starting them both in the "up" position. Within seconds Bobby had shot under, grabbed both his opponent's legs, and flipped the state champ in one quick move, pinning him. I am not exaggerating; it all happened within seconds of the ref stepping away. There was shock at first and then awe. People began to scream, not just cheer or shout, but scream—yelling, whistling, going nuts. I actually thought the roof was going to blow off the gym, it was that loud. I still get emotional thinking about it. Bobby shook hands with the former state champ, had his hand lifted by the ref, and began to run around the mat, jabbing his finger into the air and looking up. This has become the universal sign for athletes to signal thanks and glory to God. Thousands of athletes trust God for their performance each day. Some pray for safety, others pray for courage, but all rely on God's faithfulness to sustain them in the joyful heat of competition. Yes, that night ranks right up there in my heart as one of my ministry highlights. It was an awesome moment and even more so for Bobby, who experienced God's faithfulness. Faith in God's faithfulness alone doesn't ensure scoreboard success, but it does ensure a deeper walk with him, something available to each of us, regardless of athletic ability.

In the Midst of Disappointment – A Time of Grace

How do we face disappointment in assignments, relationships, or provision? I think God wants us to trust him with our plans and dreams he guides us into, but he also wants us to be more ambitious in our desire to know him and walk with him. The Bible guarantees disappointment, from Abraham to Paul. In fact, every major biblical character faced it. It's tough, but handled by faith, God uses it to build character and hope. I tell the guys, *God is not trying to jack you around, he loves you.* But he is God and we are not. His ways are higher than ours and beyond our comprehension sometimes. His goal is always to glorify the Son while conforming us to his image. In each temptation there is a way of escape. In each trial he offers wisdom to those who seek him with faith.

When our plans go off track, God is bigger. He can still

land the plane. Instead of wallowing in anger or self-pity, I try to throw myself into his presence. Praising him, thanking him, waiting for him. Often, while waiting and listening, I hear things that perhaps he has wanted to say, but no one with whom I am personally acquainted was listening. They may be unrelated to the current crisis, but not to my personal walk. Once, while fasting, I heard his voice on five things that needed to change in my life.

Ouch! I was prepped for some great unrevealed biblical truth I could use to impress others! But he quickly got my full and undivided attention about gossip, one of the five, when a coach called and confronted me for spreading a rumor about him. As soon as I heard his name, I began to apologize. (Important advice to anyone working with students: don't tell eighth-grade girls anything you don't want to go viral!) The coach graciously forgave me and later became the principal at one of the schools I visit.

God's plans for us include faith and humility and vulnerability. He will not let you walk alone, proud in your heart. You will have to ask for help. Surprisingly, others will have been waiting, placed in your life by him to help. O Saint, it is in weakness that we find our strength in him. So, in the disappointments of life, we are steered into a faith filled journey of adventure and risk, which glorifies the Son. "But he said to me, 'My grace is sufficient for you, for my power is made perfect in weakness . . .'" (2 Cor. 12:9 ESV).

Desiring God and Golf –
A Season of Freedom

This morning I am reminded of John Piper's book *Desiring God* as canine friend Hunter nuzzles me and I browse Philippians 3. It's Paul's declaration of liberty, counting all things which were said to be profitable as loss for the sake of knowing Christ.

What freedom, knowing that we can obey him simply by seeking him out and he provides the power even for this seeking out of himself! I relish the joy of seeing him in the sunrise along the bike path and in the beautiful sunset last night on the Ridgeview Ranch golf course. I was working on acknowledging his presence in my game, and though some shots were struck poorly, I maintained fellowship with him. Why does a sovereign God inject himself into an inconsequential golf game? To remind me of old truths once learned? Perhaps he just loves being with his child.

One of my hangouts is Christ Church's Men's Golf Night, a Thursday night league during daylight saving, April through September. These guys are one of my favorite foursomes of friends. We tease and encourage each other on the course and pray for each other off the course. There have been awesome prayer answers over the seasons concerning our surgeries, jobs, my ministry, our children, and a mortgage refinance.

Regular golfing amigos: (L-R ?) Me, Jeff Muenstermann, Chris Bush, Mark Glosser.

This binds us into a deeper fellowship that makes the golf more fun.

While regularly suffering through errant tee shots, I am joyfully carried along by the fellowship of my golfing companions. Yes, much like the Christian life, we can't do it alone; we need help, and even when there are painful parts of our lives, there is beauty to behold, fresh air to breath, and the challenge that we can start over on the next hole.

Discussions on the Back of a Flight – A Time of Kindness and Mercy

Ameen and his dog sat next to me on a recent flight. A God setting, so rich with conversational possibilities, that who was I to resist? Three hours later I am telling Ameen what kind of woman to marry and to stop listening to CNN. Ha! How did we get there? Through hours of listening and asking questions. Ameen was not religious, though raised in an Egyptian family. He was college educated, ran his own business, and had definite opinions of how Christian politicians should behave and how they should be more concerned about the poor. He was stuck on his ideas about minimum wage. It was clear he really didn't know any Christians or what gracious acts of mercy Christians had enacted around the world over the centuries.

So I shared a true and recent story I heard from the source. Friend Randy Creech, chaplain to the police and fire departments in a nearby suburb, related this from a recent ride with an officer. They got a call for assistance to a major North Texas intersection where a car had become stranded. The driver, a woman, couldn't find her driver's license and had run out of gas. Two small boys sat quietly in the back seat. When the officer returned to the squad car, he relayed the predicament to my friend as he pulled up her long list of prior tickets and outstanding warrants. Friend Creech asked if he would take her in. The cop replied, "How would that help the two children in the back seat?" The officer obtained gasoline for her instead, and as he left, he said, "Ma'am, you have a good day, and you might want to pay down some of those tickets so you don't get in trouble next time."

Ameen stared at me, speechless. I told him this is typical of what Christians are doing all over the world to help the poor every day. Most of us don't enact these kindnesses for public acclaim, but some should be publicized to glorify Christ. Jesus said that if he were lifted up, he would draw all men unto himself. These kindnesses (and a thousand beside) reflect Christ in our circles of influence, lifting him up for the whole world to see.

Assisting God in the Harvest –
A Season of Partnership

I absorbed a couple of days on the Rogue River in South-ern Oregon some years back while I was visiting the in-laws. That's what you do with the days here: you don't live them, you absorb them. I am twenty feet above the famous Rogue River, breathing in clean air, drinking well water (sans chemicals), eating fresh vegetables, fruit, fish, etc. Absorbing the sun by the mega ray, or however it's measured. Taking long walks past farms, horses, trees, and gardens, all framed with the beautiful backdrop of the mountains which ring the Rogue Valley. This was my thirtieth year on this river which hosted my wedding day and has been the site of countless joyful visits and mis-sionary rehabilitations ever since.

The property here is ringed with blackberry bushes. By August, the berries are ripening and ready to be snatched

Rogue River from Susie's backyard, Grants Pass, Oregon.

from their thorny lair. Blackberry picking is a bloody contact sport. These vines do not easily relinquish their bounty. I have learned much about life from the picking of these branches, which I would love to share with you.

There is an incredible amount of fruit that goes unpicked every year; it just ripens on the vine and no one ever sees it, tends it, nada. How many people are ripe, ready to hear about the love and forgiveness the Lord offers, but go unapproached? Does spiritual ripeness in people last longer, or is it seasonal, like with fruit?

Some of the best blackberries are tucked away in places that require more work and pain to reach. Why is it that most of the biggest, juiciest, ripest berries seem just beyond reach? I find myself trampling down low vines to step deeper into the prickly bush to retrieve these, and there is always a painful pricking price to be paid.

Often it takes more planning and prayer and work to get to some of the most influential people. People who have become insulated by business and scheduling . . . though they are so ready. And they appreciate the effort it takes to reach them.

Usually I find these people are amused or encouraged that someone would go to such lengths to reach them, knowing instinctively it was the Lord who pulled it off and that he cared that much. It answers questions they have about his power and love for them when we have to work to reach them.

When you have retrieved and washed your prey, you do wind up with some incredible produce. So sweet, so good, and so good for you. Sprinkled on your cereal, baked into a jam, or just eaten by hand . . . blackberries are a treat. So soldier on! It's worth the fight. Press on and work your way into the fray for that juicy reward! Yet press on even more for the harvest of souls, prepared by the Lord of the harvest: "Look unto the fields, for they are white for harvest!"

NYC Post 9/11 - A Season of Sovereignty

Like many people, I hold some fascination for New York City, the Big Apple. After 9/11, I made my third and fourth trips there to do mission work with Cru High School. These trips caused me to fall in love even more. We had the good mix of doing incredibly significant work for the gospel packaged together with great sightseeing and fellowship with some of my best and closest friends.

Many observed that after the towers fell, the disposition of the city changed. That fall, the sound of horns honking, people yelling . . . all dissipated into kindness, smiles, and a realization that life was to be appreciated, not angered through.

I got into a good conversation with my Jewish driver from LaGuardia to the hotel. Israeli he called himself, not really liking the title "Jew." When I asked why, it seemed his daughter had contracted Crohn's disease, and this had fatally wounded his Jewishness. We talked all the way and beyond as he sat in front of the Uptown Hilton and listened to some of my best encouragement and apologetics. I urged him not to give up on God. He seemed a happy, upbeat entrepreneur, having found me in the bowels of LaGuardia, persuading me to go for a ride.

In December, Cru distributed our trendy evangelistic gift bags to the students at Martin Luther King Junior High near the Lincoln Center. We had contacted a teacher who was supposed to secure permission for our distribution. Upon our arrival, there was no teacher. The police assigned to guard the school that day told us gruffly we had to have permission from the vice principal. Debbie Minell, one of my Cru colleagues, marched into the school, found the VP busy in his office, simply explained who she was, and told him that he could contact her with any questions. Boldly placing her business card on his desk, she turned and marched out before he could ask any questions. Arriving back on the sidewalk in front of the school, she told the police she had spoken to the VP, and we continued unpacking the gift bags. By now the police had seen their contents and were asking if they could have some for their kids.

Within minutes, school emptied and 1,500 bags disappeared off the sidewalk. As we cleaned up, the cops, now our friends, helped us dispose of the empty boxes. Our teacher contact appeared, assuring us we did indeed have permission. She had been called into an emergency conference in the principal's office because they had heard rumors of a riot after school. The riot never materialized. I can't be sure what difference our presence made, but I am certain it was no coincidence that God brought kids the Good News on a bad news day.

There are times in the pursuit of God's will that we will face opposition. It's a biblical guarantee. Nehemiah began rebuilding the wall around Jerusalem, and his enemies threatened to attack. He simply armed the builders and they continued to work. Construction on the wall was completed in fifty-two days, and to this day the quality and length of time it took to build that wall are considered an engineering marvel. The Lord says stand and fight in his power, don't quit. Our enemy is not flesh and blood. The cops were simply doing their job that day; they weren't the enemy. God worked it so that they became our appreciative friends and allies. Our sovereign God is at work to reach people with the Good News. Expect him to partner with you as he leads and provides and protects.

Days after a distribution at Math and Science High in East Harlem, one of our staff, Mark Sanders, was invited to speak at the same high school. Arriving early, he noticed that twenty of the thirty students were reading the paperback Bibles that we distributed in the kits weeks earlier. They had no idea he was connected to the distribution. This was just a snapshot of the impact our work had accomplished and of the victory over our enemies. I am discovering that often, when tragedy strikes, our sovereign God turns these sad circumstances into gospel opportunities. Cru High School and partners from all over the United States distributed 880,000 of these gospel gift bags to students across the five boroughs that fall . . . students who were open to spiritual answers because of 9/11.

The Love of Dogs - A Decade of His Unchanging Presence

It was hot that week in Texas, some days well over a hundred degrees. Nothing new in that. I was trying out a new regimen of walking an hour a day. My dog, Hunter, ten- and-a-half years old, had accompanied me in the late afternoon heat. He seemed a little sluggish on the way back, so we stopped for water and headed in. I was talking to friend Faulkner as we approached the house and laughing that I didn't know if we were both going to make it. As we opened the gate, I said, "Well, the dog made it."

Later, my neighbor came over and said Hunter was out. Strange, he was panting so much, I didn't expect him to leave the back porch. I went out looking, but no dog. Strange again. After a while, I got in the car to search. Neighbors had found him between houses nearby and near death. I piled him into the car and raced home, using a cold water bath to try to reduce his temperature. But all rescue efforts failed to bring him back. We buried him beneath a red oak in the backyard. For several days, a rabbit visited, sitting on his rendered mound, paying homage perhaps to a vanquished foe.

So much to say about a dog. Early on, we would return from errands to find my young son's underwear strewn about the living area. We kept after Ben about this sloppiness despite his denials . . . until we realized it was Hunter's way of punishing us for leaving him home alone. He was a people dog, exploring new relationships with everyone who came into the house. Here are some reflections on the parallels between the dog world and our world.

One morning I had followed my usual custom of venturing into the front yard at sunrise with coffee in hand to watch my Brittany roam the neighborhood in search of squirrel, rabbit, and dove. One of Hunter's worst habits was finding fresh markings from one of his canine brothers, and rubbing and driving through it till it was matted along his neck and shoulders in sort of a perverted reverse version of marking his territory. This perfumed the air with a fresh stench and drove a deep wedge between dog and master . . . and anyone else with functioning olfactory glands. In order to allow him back into the house and resume the loving relationships he enjoyed in my family, I had to bathe him outside, no matter what the temperature. We had found a wonderful dog shampoo that erased all smells, including skunk and poop.

After this time-honored ritual of bathing, I resumed my devotions that day, kneeling next to the couch. I couldn't help but notice Hunter dog seemed to be rubbing and driving along my sweatpants just like he does the neighborhood markings . . . like he was trying to pick up my scent in his fur, identifying with me. OK, Champions for Christ . . . most of you can see where this is going.

On another day, soon after the dog shampooing episode, I awoke too early, all the guts and gore from the previous night's TV viewing cascading front and center onto my cranial big screen. I stopped and confessed this poor use of time and mind warping . . . and couldn't wait to rise up, coffee up, and get into the Word, cleansing the crap with God's odor-removing shampoo of 1 John 1:9, reaffirming my child/Father relationship in this family of faith which I love, rubbing and driving into the truth of my position in him secured by Christ's sacrifice till it perfumed the air around me. I once again identified with Christ in whom I rest secure. I know what this incredible God is like because his attributes never change and his blessings are new every morning. Special thanks to Zeke Zeiler, who taught me to pay attention to dogs.

Yours for a closer walk and cleaner dogs!

Hunter on a quail hunt, Rio Vista Ranch.

On Battles, Leadership and God's Glory – A Time of Purpose

The service academies, like the Air Force's, train leaders. Our son, Ben, attended classes and read numerous books on the subject. He believes you best learn leadership by watching people in authority over you. You then cull out the bad and keep the rest. Or, we could just watch "Band of Brothers," the true story of the 82nd Airborne's Company E. For my money, Captain Dick Winters' true story portrays an incredible model of leadership. Ben and I believe that apart from biographies, you don't get it totally by studying books.

Someone has to lead men into battle. Some wars have to be fought, and I have been engaged in an ongoing spiritual battle over the souls of students. Men are created to fight for things.

They fight for their wives, their teams, their friends, their jobs, their dreams, and their countries. Some lead better in peace than in war. Some, like Churchill, Patton, and Eisenhower, are wartime leaders.

Rick Atkinson's book *An Army at Dawn* is the first of his trilogy on World War II. He meticulously describes General Eisenhower's growth as a wartime leader, much of which was the result of on the job training. Really, like, where is the Allied Commander training school for participation in world wars? Trying to appease the French and British allies while getting throttled by the weather, terrain, and Germans in North Africa was a baptism by fire. Eisenhower was reticent and slow in making decisions. Patton and others doubted and criticized him. But Ike learned quickly, persevering through initial losses to become the famous war hero and Allied commander we celebrate now. How would you like to have Winston Churchill and Franklin D. Roosevelt looking over your shoulder while you fought Rommel in the deserts of North Africa?

Leaders should be driven by vision, but always with the consideration for the state of their troops. Washington led his ragtag group of revolutionaries miles through blowing snow across a frozen river at night on Christmas Day to attack the Hessians in Trenton. It was his first victory after being chased across Brooklyn, Manhattan, New Jersey, and into Pennsylvania. His men perhaps needed the confidence gained in the victory more than shoes, of which many were bereft. This leadership is legendary and foundational to American life. Yet we don't always fight the Hessians. Peacetime leadership requires its own set of nuances. Balancing training, equipping, and vision-casting along with preparing for battle. This all falls on leadership, and those who lead best know and care about their people. God handpicked and empowered biblical leaders like Abraham and David. Each gave glory to the Lord, sometimes before and sometimes after battles. David tells Saul, "The Lord who delivered me from the paw of the lion and from the paw of the bear will deliver me from the hand of this Philistine." When the Lord leads us into battle, we have the assurance he is with us, fighting for us.

With this assurance men and women of God have stepped into arenas of battle for centuries, willing to risk all that the Lord would be glorified, his purposes accomplished.

Shared Suffering at the YMCA – A Time for Mercy

We are avid YMCA people. Going four to six times a week, we work out in a family atmosphere, where we have made some great friends. I even performed a marriage as a result of "Y" friendships. This keeps us young. One morning I was approached by one of my Y friends. He told me that I reminded him of his heart doctor, and each time he sees me, it urges him to follow his doctor's instructions. He is from India, and that day he asked me what I did for work. After explaining a little about being a missionary, he asked me some questions. *Why did his granddaughter have to die so young? Why does God allow things like the death of a child?*

Wow! Hoping my coffee was still working and shooting up some quick prayers, I asked him if he really wanted a biblical answer. He said yes. I expressed sorrow for his loss, not wanting to justify God's position or participation in a child's death too quickly. The good news is that God doesn't need my skills as an apologist, but people suffer so, and I hate it when they blame God. Ultimately, who else is there to blame?

Sadly, many of these same suffering people didn't think to attribute their blessings to God, only their losses. But, being that as it is with all of us self-centered people, my dear friend was really looking for answers, and anything I can do to point people to God's love and forgiveness, I will.

I started with a perfect world and a perfect garden in Genesis and worked through the fall of man and the resulting curse on planet Earth. Bad things happen to all of us, and even God the Father suffered the death of his Son so that there could be ultimate answers to suffering.

My friend told me Hindus think we suffer as a result of sins in a past life. Christianity teaches only one life here, but another one to come without suffering and pain. Being Earth-centric, we ask, *why suffering?* Yet believing in a world to come gives meaning to suffering. C. S. Lewis addresses the subject better than most in his book *The Problem of Pain,* and I also recommend his friend Sheldon Vanauken's book *A Severe Mercy*; both give deep and wonderful explanation to encourage the reader.

Personally, I have found suffering to be such a hassle! And it certainly doesn't fit into our concept of the American Dream or the Christian version of the American Dream. The awful truth is that one of God's favorite growth tools is suffering. After all, our hero and Savior suffered, and as we walk with him, we should expect that our path will also include suffering. You can trace out the suffering of almost every biblical character, which is why they had character.

When Ananias was being recruited to participate in Saul's conversion, he thought the Lord was a little confused about

Saul's identity. He heard back from God in Acts 9:15–16: "Go, for he is a chosen instrument of mine to carry my name before the Gentiles and kings and the children of Israel. For I will show him how much he must suffer for the sake of my name."

Part of the deal for Saul was suffering. Later, he writes in Philippians 3:10–11 "that I may know him and the power of his resurrection, and may share his sufferings, becoming like him in his death, that by any means possible I may attain the resurrection from the dead."

Once we come to peace with the fact that suffering is part of this incredible new life, and that whatever comes our way is divinely and lovingly orchestrated and overseen, we can trust him with it. Susie and I have suffered as most couples our age with loss of family and friends, heartaches over hurt children and lost students, feeling misunderstood, underappreciated, and overlooked. I guess you could classify suffering into categories. Some of what we experience would be called first-world problems compared to the Syrian refugees' problems. But my suffering is what the Lord gave me to suffer. And I have developed lots of coping mechanisms like ignoring it, shopping, exercising, snacking, or focusing on something else. My number one coping skill? Complaining and whining.

I have perfected and polished up all of these. When Paul asked God to take away his suffering, he was informed that he was stronger because of it and that God's grace was sufficient. Don't be afraid to be honest with God about how you feel. He can handle our anger and tears. But be sure to circle around to passages like Psalm 23, Romans 8, Matthew 11:28–31, and plenty of others. His Word breathes hope into our hearts, stirs up faith, and corrects perspective. The book of Job chronicles incredible suffering, for which Job never got an explanation. God is God and not required to explain himself, though graciously, he often does. Sometimes the explanation comes in hindsight, sometimes it comes in silence. Suffering makes us real: it broadens our faith and draws us deeper into his arms. And as we suffer, we are comforted knowing that he purposes circumstances which just seem senseless and hurtful and gives his Spirit to comfort and guide.

Chris and I shared many conversations at the Y subsequent to that one. My friend had been attending church with his daughter, and this former petroleum engineer from India acknowledged that it encouraged him to know that God suffered too. Sometimes the YMCA provides me with more than just a physical workout.

The Fleeting Nature of Fame – A Moment of Humility

When Heather, our oldest, was ready for college, we couldn't find a fit for her in Texas, so we settled on Seattle. It was far away, completely different, and therefore a great choice in so many ways. She loved her time at Seattle Pacific University, and we loved visiting her each year. This day finds me in Wallingford, one neighborhood west of the University of Washington. Susie's cousin lives there and we often stayed with her. Built in the'20s, this amalgamation of Arts and Crafts homes are perched on a hillside overlooking downtown Seattle and Lake Union. At the base of the hill, on the water, lies Gas Works Park, where, as it happened, I met Dave Matthews. This beautiful grassy park is just the place to hang out and picnic as you watch kayakers rowing by or tourists boarding pontoon planes for a trip downtown. My daughter and I were picnicking there, and just as I began to drift off, she grabbed me and said, "Dad! Was that Dave Matthews you were talking to?" (Dave is a famous rocker for those uneducated in pop culture.)

"Sure, honey, whatever, like I would know Dave Matthews if I saw him . . ."

"Yes, Dad, that was him—he has two little daughters just like that! Everyone just treats him like he's normal, which is what is so cool about Seattle, they don't bother their celebrities."

And so, evidently, I had been very Seattle-ish, talking to Dave Matthews like he was just another guy, which of course, he is: just another guy who performs in front of tens of thousands of people every year and then wonders out loud if a pontoon plane just took off from Lake Union in front of Gas Works Park and asks a total stranger about it.

Which reminds me of another of my numerous brushes with fame, which happened in New York City's neighborhood of Chelsea somewhere in the mid-twenties at a trendy restaurant (aren't they all?!). While working our Cru outreach to students in the Big Apple after 9/11, I took some time to visit a former student from Plano, Bo Collins, who had moved there for work in the financial district. Bo had heard the first jetliner hit the tower and had stepped onto the front of the New York Mercantile Exchange with his building supervisor to witness the second crash. They immediately emptied their guys onto ferries to New Jersey, thinking there might be more planes hitting buildings.

We went out to this fun place around the corner from his home and saw Jonathan Price come in with friends after we had been served. Price has played the villain in James Bond movies, done classy Jaguar commercials, and a host of other gigs. Of course, everyone noticed him when he came in.

Strangely, each time I happened to glance over to check on him, he was checking on me. We were laughing a little loudly over old Plano stories, which may have initially caught his attention. But no kidding, even Bo picked up on it. "Look at Jonathan Price," I said. "He thinks he recognizes me, but he's not certain it's really me!" I am guessing this is one of the things celebrities say to each other when they think they have been spotted by their fans.

Not many of us are slated for celebrity status, aside from Andy Warhol's future prediction of fifteen minutes of fame for everyone. Yet we are guaranteed 24/7 attention from the other side of eternity, which is far more valuable, assuring, and humbling. In Psalm 139:17 David says, "How precious are your thoughts about me, O God. They cannot be numbered! I can't even count them; they outnumber the grains of sand! And when I wake up, you are still with me!"

Whether we find ourselves well known or little known, we each have a significant role to play. The Sovereign Lord dishes out these roles and gifts to us to be accomplished by faith as part of his body, the church. He does provide an occasional snapshot of our impact, just enough encouragement and affirmation to keep us going, but certainly not fame. I would join the John the Baptist's "Humble Camp," proclaiming, "He must increase, but I would decrease" (John 3:30 NASB).

From Little to Big – A Lifetime with an Unchanging God

I like to start with the little and work up to the big. If God is concerned about the little, how much more is he concerned about the grand? Post college, as a newly revived believer, I had perfected, with much consternation, an incredible tee shot. This stroke sent my first shot of each hole down the fairway for eighty yards or so and then, *boom*, ninety degrees right, delivering my ball two or three fairways away. In the vernacular of golf; a duck slice, quick fade . . . which was what I did to Colonial Country Club . . . a quick fade. My father received a membership to Colonial through a new job when I was in high school. I promptly marched my little municipal course game out onto the hallowed grounds of the National Invitational, home of Ben Hogan's trophies and triumphs. My pride was soon mashed.

The humility of having foursomes of older women ask to play through as I wondered off sideways in search of my ball was more than my ego could handle. Humbly retreating back to the local municipal courses, I began to think, *Why not pray about this tee shot?* One afternoon at the Boaz Course in West Ft. Worth, I began to pray about each shot. Why shouldn't I enjoy the Lord's company all the way around the course? My well-honed monstrosity of a slice disappeared that day to never, ever return. I went away thinking, *If God cares enough to work on my golf game, how much more does he care about the more important things in my life?* And thus began the adventure of a constant journey from little to big, appreciating his attention to the little things of life while trying to trust him to accomplish the big.

Recently, while playing with my son-in-law and a couple of longtime friends, I hit my first hole in one. Witnesses were long time golfing buddies Mark Glosser, a major contributor to the publishing of Tales and Stan Fischer. Having no expectations of grandeur on that par 3, I had ducked down in search of my favorite tee when the yelling commenced. By the time I rose up, my ball had disappeared. This rare and exciting event, though just a side note in the annals of golf, counted for so much more in my journey of faith. The Lord loves to surprise us with gifts. I was just thankful for fellowship with friends on a fun course. God chose to bless me beyond the fellowship. I did nothing to deserve it.

In the clubhouse afterwards, Fischer began explaining how we could shadow box that ball and mount it along with the scorecard for a nice wall display. I looked at him incredulously. "What ball? You never told me to save the ball! I lost it on the next hole!"

That story continues to illicit laughter among the group. It's just some of the joy of friendship with other men which God intends, I believe, for the building up of the saints. Men need other good men in their lives, and I have been blessed in friendships, from little to big, all at the hands of a gracious, loving Father.

From Matthew 6, Jesus encourages us from little to big in his comparisons between us and birds and grassy flowers. If he will take care of them, how much more will he take care of us? We need not worry, but we can anticipate his provision as we move in our faith from little to big:

"But if God so clothes the grass of the field, which today is alive and tomorrow is thrown into the oven, will he not much more clothe you, O you of little faith? Therefore do not be anxious, saying, 'What shall we eat?' or 'What shall we drink?' or 'What shall we wear?' For the Gentiles seek after all these things, and your heavenly Father knows that you need them all. But seek first the kingdom of God and his righteousness, and all these things will be added to you."
—MATTHEW 6:30–33

Appreciation of Gardens –
A Season of His Omnipresence

We joined friends on the shores of Dallas's White Rock Lake in the mid '80s to watch the sunset and enjoy a Fourth of July fireworks display. Years later, friend Bob Simmons would share how much he loved visits to the Dallas Arboretum with his son William. I vaguely placed it in the same area as White Rock Lake.

One of my best discoveries was returning to White Rock several years ago with my staff for a Christmas display at the DeGoyler Estate. It got me into the Arboretum and hooked. Now, most Friday mornings you can find me here after the infamous Buckaroo Bible Study. I haunt the park benches, annoy the squirrels, and meet with God. What a great place to pray and meditate, in the manicured beauty of a garden. Hmm, wonder whose idea that was initially?

I have fun dodging the legions of elementary school kids who descend upon the park in bright yellow school buses. Their teachers try to instill some modicum of order and decorum, but little boys can't contain themselves. They know they are home somehow. Deep in their genetics, they are caught up in the wonder of the trees and streams.

Entering the gardens one mild day in September, I am bum-rushed by the colors of late summer. The park is quiet and beautiful. The air of morning is freshened after some good rains. A dry cool front caresses the city, post Hurricane Ike.

Could it be there are more colors in late summer than during the Arboretum's touted "Dallas Blooms"? I take time to embrace this dear old friend. Like a well-kept secret, in the early mornings of the garden you can imagine the Lord's handiwork in the first garden. Didn't Adam cultivate and work with the Lord in the garden? Pruning, harvesting, and enjoying the work that now is the bane of many weekend warriors? Oh, yeah, the bugs, thorns, and weeds came after the nibbling of forbidden fruit.

Feeling at home in a garden, whether it's my backyard, the Arboretum, or the wilds of Texas, I have always been drawn outside. On hunts I like to sit down by a tree, close my eyes, and just listen. Perhaps listening is my lost art. A friend told me of a daily devotion that requires two minutes of listening twice during the lesson. Surely the Lord has much to say to us which goes unheard, whether in a garden or indoors. He pulled the disciples away for times alone, away from the crowds. In Matthew 11:28–30 he calls, "Come to me, all of you who are weary and carry heavy burdens, and I will give you rest. Take my yoke upon you. Let me teach you, because I am humble and gentle at heart, and you will find rest for your souls. For my yoke is easy to bear, and the burden I give you is light."

Great passages like these deserve a hearing, even a long meditation. And in hearing we begin to relax in his Spirit, knowing the omnipresent God of Creation speaks clearly to the hearts. He is in the garden, the garage, the kitchen, the office, the fields, and the schools, speaking peace and courage to our hearts in ways only he can.

The Great Outdoors – A Session with His Goodness

Prior to the advent of children, Susie and I decided we would be a family that camped. Current research shows there are lots of benefits besides no sleep, porta-potties, and cold food. For years, we camped late fall and early spring with the Adkison crew, whether we needed it or not. We hit every state park within a two-hour radius of the Metroplex and doubled up on some around Lake Texoma. We included some other good friends who showed up with a three-legged pink stool and suitcases. This didn't go down without an appropriate amount of teasing and laughter. Ha! These are great memories for our family and served as a bonding agent for us.

Since this worked so well with my family, I decided it would be good for my staff team. We had several forced marches into eastern Oklahoma. One reluctant staff couple brought their mattress from home. The first morning, I noticed it sticking out through the front door of their tent. The next year, they inherited a VW camper, which they insisted was the same as tent camping. In order to keep the peace, I reluctantly agreed.

Friend Rob Farrell has opened his arms wide to our work with students since the mid '80s, and we have swarmed upon his ranch like the locusts of Old Testament stories with our tents and an old school bus we borrowed from the Baptists. What adventures! I actually never rode in that bus; thanks be to God! One year the bus wouldn't start in the Prairie Creek church parking lot. Freshly equipped after seminars on spiritual warfare, we boldly laid hands on the hood, praying against the Evil One and invoking the Lord's help. The engine roared to life and off we went!

Another year, we took kids to Steve Cooper's family farm south of Brownwood, where the bus was hijacked by a couple of good old boys who had been out rabbit hunting. Tossing their fresh bloody kill across the hood, they boarded the bus with shotguns at the ready. Tobacco juice dripped down their chins onto their bare chests and bib overalls.

Our staff guy driving the bus knew they were volunteers, but the kids were panicked. The hillbillies demanded to know who the kids were and what they were doing! One brave kid blurted out, in his best falsetto voice, "We're just a bunch of C-C-Christian kids on a c-c-campout!!"

Well, the good ole boys went ballistic with threats and shouting, questioning their Christianity. They then took them to see their Pa. The students didn't recognize Cru Dallas staff Steve "Coop" Cooper in the role of "Pa," because they were convinced they were going to die. The skit had all been staged by a couple of volunteers the kids hadn't met, Pete Henning and Johnny Polk (Johnny, the longtime camp director at TBarM). When I arrived late the next morning, all I heard was, "Benton! That wasn't funny!"

I had no idea about the impromptu skit or the gravity of it. The volunteers had figured the kids would laugh them off the bus, but when that didn't happen, they just strung it out. Of course, afterwards, one the guys, Marshall Jackson, claimed they were planning to jump the hillbillies, but guys can talk, especially high school guys! It was an awesome weekend of fishing and swimming in a creek, working through an obstacle course we set up, playing tennis ball guerrilla warfare, square dancing under the stars, and Bible studies. What did the kids remember? What was all they talked about for months? The hijacking, of course!

Convinced that campouts provide a fun setting for spiritual impact, I continue to take guys at least once a year. From a guy chasing girls with an axe to copperheads under tents, night hikes in the woods, football games in the Brazos, and huge bonfires (compliments of now Dallas Police Department officer Chris Cooley), our stories are legend and provide the fun necessary to sustain a high school ministry. Putting city boys into the woods is almost magical, like the release of some ancient DNA that has been cooped up and unrecognizable. They never want to leave; they know somehow they have come home and that they are free to be themselves. The goodness of God is on display in the beauty of nature. We don't really need these beautiful vistas and sunsets, do we? What function do they play? All I can figure is they just point us to the goodness of God. God is good.

As we grow in faith, the Spirit frees us up and unlocks our ancient longing to connect with our good Father. We are free to be ourselves, sharing his love without concern for the judgments of others. Whether in the cities or in the country, Christ is lifted up best by those who love and serve others without thought of reputation, considering the needs of others as more important than their own.

Trumping our Stubbornness – A Nod to His Faithfulness

How old are we when God ceases to teach and correct? It must be somewhere past eighty-five. When my mom was eighty-six years old, she had a tiff with an old friend on the phone. She was reluctant to call back, feeling she had been offended on the last call. She thought she had the right to give up, justified before the Lord to call it a day in that relationship.

Guess the Lord didn't see it that way; he kept urging her to pick up the phone.

The Lord doesn't give up on us, even when he may be justified. When we have rejected him for the umpteenth time, refusing to listen, he faithfully continues to walk us past so many beautiful roses that we can't help but catch a faint whiff. In North Dallas, he drives his coffee-loving children past countless Starbucks. His love wafts by so adroitly that we cannot miss it. He stalks us lovingly, coaxing us to try again, telling us, "Don't give up." He whispers to our hearts, "I am working here with you and not just on the other end of the line."

My mom? Well, she pushed through and called again. Victory! And yet, when we don't respond to his loving, faithful wooing, when that doesn't work, he can employ the shove. There are some classic shoves, like on the CBS program "NCIS." The lead character, Mark Harmon, regularly slaps Detective Anthony D'Nozo on the back of the head, saying, "Do you think?!"

The Lord shoves us as if to say, "Hey, pal, what are you doing? Are you heading off this morning without me?"

Yikes! When you are far enough along with Christ to get messages like these, some heartfelt repentance would be a good response. Repentance means to turn from something. In our case it means to turn back toward our faithful God, humbly acknowledging our self-centeredness and submitting ourselves to his love and grace. This repositioning takes moments and reinstalls Christ as the Lord of our lives.

As we tackle our personal relationships by faith in his power to reconcile us, we experience his peace and forgiveness. It may have to be a daily ritual for some of placing relationships on his altar, acknowledging we have no right to any expectations other than his grace. These healings come in his timing; they are not dictated by us.

But as his love is poured out in our hearts, we find that he works with us and that his load is light and the yoke is easy. We aren't alone . . . ever. These relationships are at the top of his priority list for us, far above our important projects and presentations, and they all hang on him. He is able and willing to help us and heal relationships, and so, we repent. Our hearts find rest in him, the one who matches rejection with forgiveness. "Father, forgive them for they don't know what they are doing" (Luke 23:34).

My mom's friend has since passed away. They remained reconciled until her passing. Friends for years, they had become best friends later in life, attending Bible studies, playing bridge, and living and dining together at Trinity Terrace. Mom visited her daily as death approached. She has two beautiful white porcelain angels on the night stand by her bed. "That's me and Gail," she says, "I miss her every day." And because of God's graceful reconciliation, it is a missing with no regrets.

On Living a Life of Adventure – A Season of Sovereignty

Years ago, one of my roommates and friends joined the National Guard as an Airborne Ranger. He liked to sing their song, "I want to be an Airborne Ranger, I want to live a life of danger!" This song is like our song: we are airborne sometimes, sometimes left afoot, but always living our God-appointed life of danger and adventure. This fires me up: the thought that our sovereign God has chosen us for lives of adventure in his service. "For we are his workmanship, created in Christ Jesus for good works . . ." (Eph. 2:10).

My son flies V-22 Ospreys for the Air Force. Where does that leave the rest of us earthbound schmucks? Still in the life of adventure that the Lord ordains. Many of our lives will mirror George Bailey in Frank Capra's *It's a Wonderful Life* or Professor Chipping in *Goodbye Mr. Chips*. Men and women who go about life, doing ordinary things. They coach Little League, teach Sunday school, run PTA, help neighbors in distress, and suffer indignities silently, believing the best in people. Our risk-taking could include lovingly confronting a family member or neighbor, visiting one of our child's teachers for an explanation, asking for a raise, asking a company for a donation for your favorite charity, going back to school as an adult, speaking up at a zoning board hearing . . . any number of things that would get your blood pressure up for brief moments!

Yet any and all of these carried out in faith and with love, under the care and direction of our sovereign and watchful God, all qualify as adventure. Daring to initiate a spiritual conversation with a friend, going to God on your knees on behalf of a friend or on a personal issue, or daring to go deep with this incredible unknowable God who asks us to seek him. All these are part of the adventure. How else do we see God at work, without initiating something out of need?

Marching through Stages of Life – An Era of Faithful Presence

Turning sixty-six this year is a rush, but into *what*? The bathroom for one! Wow! Sixty and still wearing jeans! Fifty years ago, this was unthinkable. The Gap is shopping central for many boomers still clinging to some modicum of lost youth in cotton.

But as I watch the older crew age beautifully, I often ask myself, *Do I really want to live that long?* I recently told the Lord, *I don't want to live another twenty years unless they are productive.* How silly. I am sure he feels the same way!

Certainly God has purpose for us, no matter what the age. I would be one of the Calebs of my generation. Caleb was one of the Israelis who left Egypt with Moses and traveled through the desert to the Promised Land. He was forty when they departed, eighty when they arrived. He and Joshua had presented an assessment of the Jew's chances for acquiring an occupied land that took into account the fear of the Lord, a sovereign God. But theirs was the minority report; it took forty years of wilderness roaming to get back around to the Promised Land.

At eighty-five, he was ready to fight for the fulfillment of what the Lord had promised. In short, Caleb would not compromise one step from the purposes of God. It wasn't about selfish ambition, it was about so much more. Caleb was about serving God, Yahweh, Adonai . . . no one else deserved the service of this focused man. In Joshua 14:8, Caleb says, "yet I wholly followed the Lord my God."

His faithfulness calls out to my soul. His purposes may change, but they will always be his purposes, and like Peter when cornered by one of Jesus's tough questions, I say, "Lord, where else would I go? You have brought me to know you as Lord, and you alone have the words of eternal life."

Isn't it just an easy conclusion that the Lord has purpose for us at every age? Good grief, we aren't like racehorses put out to pasture after brilliant or not so brilliant careers. Bob Buford's book *Halftime* offers some great strategies to encourage men to stay the course and search out new ways to serve the Lord at middle age.

Stages of Life

Robert Clinton, a professor at Fuller Seminary in Pasadena, writes in his book on leadership that we move through stages if we continue to walk with the Lord. He and his grad students studied the lives of men from the Bible, post-Bible histories of men of faith, and current leaders of faith. Many of Clinton's students were clergy who had fallen in some way and wanted to get back into the game, believing that we serve a God of second chances. Their findings were so encouraging to me. They were looking to discover if there were any general patterns to lives of men who served God, whether in ministry or industry or education, whatever the profession. And they bingoed! Of course, there is no exact roadmap other than to follow paths of faith, love, and hope in all good humility.

But they saw there were general stages men could expect the Lord to lead them through. As young guys in the work, we are full of passion and vinegar, running on high octane, pedal to the metal, but only banging on 5 to 6 of the cylinders of our 8-cylinder transport. As we continue to seek him in faithful obedience, he wears off rough edges and teaches us submission to his ordained order in our lives. He urges us to reach for our dreams and love him as we serve in his almighty power. He positions us in the places he has preordained for us before the beginning of time. Ephesians 2 says he has prepared good works for us to walk in . . . and what promise this communicates to us!

One of the last stages Clinton researched is the mentor or consultant stage. I find myself sliding into this stage in youth ministry, just by the sheer weight of years of faithful service survived with good humor and much self-deprecation. Learning discretion has been one of my toughest lessons. As a Sanguine, I like to experience life, laugh about it, share it, and forget it. But I am learning that some things are better left unsaid. Period. Amen.

So I embrace this next stage in my great adventure, and as I run into this high garden, I look around to see other faithful saints running abreast of me and before me, serving gladly into older ages. My admiration goes to public figures like Ronald Reagan, John Wooden, Bill Bright, and personal friends Steve Thomas, George Gillen, Barry Wood, Jerry Green, and Jim Williams who still pursue their dreams, unhindered by age.

Leadership at Altitude –
A Time of Spiritual Authority

Estes Park is beautifully snuggled into the Rocky Mountain National Park, making the Continental Divide visible everywhere. I fell in love with my wife there in the'70s, during our first stateside summer projects. They were great summers, as we were breaking ground in youth work. They were exciting days.

My first summer in Estes, I lived in a converted garage with two college guys and three high school guys. Three sets of bunk beds and a bathroom so small you could shower, shave, and do your business concurrently. Weeks into the project, we imposed a curfew. This move was not well received. It was like a mutiny in our cabin, which we had named the Sugar Shack. I found myself hiking a mile away each morning to spend time with God. Somehow I was given Watchman Nee's book *Spiri-*

tual Authority during this trying time. One night, during our evening discussions in the Sugar Shack, I told the guys with much fear and trembling and tears that God had placed me in authority over them for the summer. I acknowledged that I wasn't perfect, but as far as leadership in the Sugar Shack, I was the guy.

Their response to this emboldened speech was more than I could have hoped. Their anger and resentment melted into humility and reconciliation. One of them wondered how he could have treated me that way, since I was one of his best friends. After the emotional release of the evening and a good night's rest, I found myself sitting on the front porch as I finished my devotions the next day, not a mile away.

Later that summer, as curfew approached one night, I began to sense some trouble in my spirit. Three of us began to pray for the other two boys who were still out. The Lord impressed on us that something big was going down and we needed to pray against it in the authority of the Lord. We labored hard in prayer for the two missing in action for some time until we heard the front door open and they came crashing through and onto their bunks, astonished.

One of the first things they said was, "Were you guys praying for us?" As they relayed their part of the story, it was clear the Lord had been at work. They had met up in town with two local high school girls for dates and had wound up at one of their homes. It seems these gals were ready, willing, and able to indulge our heroes in the ways of the world. Just when the green light had been turned on and all signals were go, the guys sensed the presence of the Lord in such a powerful way of conviction that they both simultaneously jumped up and called it a night, insisting these local ladies of willingness take them home. Upon further trading of notes, we discovered that the moment of conviction coincided exactly with the timing of our prayers of authority over them and against the Evil One. There was much rejoicing that night in the Sugar Shack over the Lord's work, each student experiencing the fear of our omniscient Lord in this instance and the joy in his personal care, love, and intervention.

Spiritual Authority at Sea Level

My first lesson in spiritual authority had come in '73, in Tampa, Florida, where Cru conducted three consecutive student conferences on the USF campus. One evening, we were battling some kids who wouldn't submit to curfew and kept sneaking into each other's dorm rooms. Finding myself without bullets, I didn't know how we were going to enforce any rules, being a complete newbie at my first summer conference. One of the older staff guys, Enoch Williams, emerged from his room in his tighty-whities and, towering over this recalcitrant kid, told him that if he continued to disobey, they would put him on a Greyhound that night and send him packing. I stood amazed at this revelation of authority and watched the kid saunter off to his proper room.

This was a watershed moment for me. I asked Enoch how this worked, and he assured me of the seriousness of this threat. Equipped with the knowledge of this seemingly nuclear endgame, I have found ways to corral our late-night cowboys for years with a smile and firmness. Knowing that a quick trip home is a final and sure justice (which can be executed in the appropriate circumstance) is like owning a hybrid golf club that gets you out of trouble. It's always in your bag when you need it. I have not sent anyone home in forty-plus years—but I would!

Spiritual Authority –
A Life Empowered by Humility

That same summer in Tampa, the staff were worn out after three straight weeks of conferences and, for our last week, we welcomed 357 wild kids from Chicago. Our defenses were down and these kids were there to push the limits. There was tension from the beginning, and the campers weren't happy.

A couple days into the week, the university came to us with a couple hundred pounds of leftover watermelons. Someone came up with the idea of marching the kids across campus to eat them. So we cooked up an elaborate drama to dispense the melons.

We seated the kids on the grass between the dorms. They had no idea what was going on. As they waited, the melodrama began to unfold. On a second story breezeway in front of them, Colonel Duncan Gibbs stepped out dressed like Colonel Sanders of KFC fame. He began a conversation with his daughter, played by Mary Nell Quarles. Playing the role of his top ranch hand, I rushed in from offstage with the news that there was an Indian uprising stirring.

As the drama unfolds, Colonel Gibbs tells me to round up the boys. That was the cue for thirty of the staff guys to come flying out of a side door onto the grass, all dressed up like cowboys and riding stick horses for all they were worth. They rode around these astonished, mouth-gaping kids and formed two lines . . . marching them clear across campus while seriously playing out this skit all the way.

Arriving at a stand of live oaks, the kids spot the watermelon all cut up and laid out on tables underneath a large banner announcing the "Colonel Duncan Gibbs' Rooting Tooting' High-Falootin' Watermelon Bash." Two of the staff, dressed in full Indian regalia, welcomed the troop and made peace with Colonel Gibbs and his daughter. Lots of fun melon chomping and seed spitting ensued as did a funny thing I had not expected . . . the cessation of hostilities with the kids.

Our total and unabashed humiliation in the course of the melodrama had quelled the raging beast inside them. It had won them over, proving to them that we really cared about them and would go to great lengths to ensure they had a good conference. This was another giant lesson in my youth work development. You could have all the great speakers and musicians, which we had; the best discipleship training, which we had; and some of the most fruitful outreaches, (yes, which we had); but the strength of our work was in humility. Any correlation of this story to Jesus humbly washing the disciples' feet prior to the Last Supper or the humiliation of being flogged and crucified buck naked for the sins of the world is merely coincidental. Biblical humility ain't for the faint at heart; it's only adequately carried off in the power of the Holy Spirit and for his purposes.

"Take My yoke upon you and learn from Me, for I am gentle and humble in heart and you will find rest for your souls."
—MATTHEW 11:29 NASB

Witnessing at the Purdue Laundry Mat – A Session of Partnering

Days later, as everything wound down in Tampa, several of us caravanned up to Atlanta for a short-term assignment till our annual staff training began at Purdue. I remember this trip because we shared Christ boldly with everyone we met at restaurants and gas stations along the way. My friend Ed Smith drove a Chevy Impala convertible with the top down. Heading north, we drove into a rain shower. He passed my Camaro with a smile on his face. We broke down laughing because the direction of the rain and speed of his car combined to produce the perfect shield, preventing rain from coming into the passenger compartment. Ed just cruised by, happy as a clam, top down, smiling all the way.

That summer was like magic to me. I recall so many details, perhaps because it was my first summer with Cru. The July nights in West Lafayette were stifling in our un-air-conditioned dorms. All the guys left their doors open at night, praying for some whiff of a breeze to drift through, with no concern about possible thefts. Even though my bicycle had been stolen from the USF dorms that summer, my doors were wide open too.

Standing at Ready

My fellow teammate from TCU Cru, Doug MacFarlane, had been assigned to campus staff in California and had fallen in love there, only to have his heart broken at Purdue. Late one night, while Doug was sadly alone, doing his laundry, the Lord nudged him to speak to a couple of guys in the laundromat. Doug wanted to refuse, wallowing in his one man pity party, but faithfully obeyed. As it happens, these two guys were ripe and hungry for God, and both trusted him that night. Another great lesson went down on the ledger for me as Doug excitedly recounted the story. This incredible God we serve is apt to tear up his invitation to our pity party and give us assignments we don't feel like doing. Assignments which might result in someone's salvation. Imagine that! The next week, I sat in the same laundromat at night doing my cleaning. The Lord nudged me to talk with the biggest hairiest guy I had seen in years. With faith in hand, I followed through. I recall he was open and interested, and I was amazed and amused. What a joy to be used by the Lord while watching your laundry spinning around in a dryer. Stay ready . . . you never know when you might be nudged!

Enjoying Athletics – An Occasion for Humility

As I am covering lessons in humility, it moves me to speak of our staff conference football games. Early in the mornings or late afternoons, several of us at the Purdue training would play touch football. I had enjoyed years of playing touch as a TCU frat boy, and later, at Texas, it became a nightly ritual. So, thinking highly of my skills and loving the competition, I threw myself into these games. One afternoon I was assigned with covering Rich Magee from the campus ministry. I didn't know any of the guys in these games, having joined staff mid-year with a small group, and it being my first full staff conference. Rich was taller than me and there was nothing I could do to keep him from catching passes . . . all afternoon. As insignificant as this seems, it did serve to bolster my humility, at which point in my young Christian life and career seemed to lag hopelessly behind a burgeoning pride.

Rich and I both wound up working in Dallas with Cru. Trading notes some twenty years later, I asked Rich if he recalled the game that afternoon at Purdue. He remembered it well, because, he said, it was his best game of touch ever; he sensed he could catch anything that day. He had never had a game like it before . . . or since! Well, I informed him, I was the one he kept catching passes over, and I could not recall a game before or since where I had done so poorly! Funny how the Lord works.

First Peter 5:5-7 states: "God is opposed to the proud and exalts the humble. Humble yourselves therefore, under the hand of almighty God that he may exalt you at the proper time, casting all your anxiety on Him for he cares for you."

The connection between anxiety and pride is clear. When we are working under our own steam, pride takes over, which leads to anxiety. When we humbly submit our plans and dreams and relationships to him and live by faith, things run so much better. We get exalted . . . which could mean exonerated, promoted, or encouraged by him, all in the proper time. Christ was exalted to his current place in heaven, seated on a throne next to the Father, running the universe at the proper time. All this after the cross. So when the Bible says he cares for you, you can rest in the assurance that he is running our lives with the same power and authority he runs the universe.

Starting on Campus –
A Year of Powerful Partnership

Nobody likes rejection: it's tough on the self-concept, yet it can produce fire in the belly. Such is the case of my work at Boulder High. Above the front door are two carvings the students refer to as Jake and Minnie. They greet everyone who enters. Upon arriving in Boulder in the dead of winter '73, my first Cru high school assignment, I drove to campus on a snowy Sunday to check out my first official battlefield. The city was covered in white, quiet and still. All I recall were the two statuettes atop the main entrance and the leafless trees. The entire city looked and felt brown and white. Dennis Rainey was my first director, and had just married Barbara the previous summer. Dennis worked Fairview High School and I worked Boulder High till he got promoted nine months later, and I took his place as city director.

Dennis put me in charge of hosting a performance by Andre' Kole, Cru's illusionist evangelist. I had helped promote Andre' at TCU as a volunteer, and thought I had matters well in hand until I was questioned in a staff meeting about details. Dennis more than adequately exposed the flaws in my procrastination. Discipline is a wonderful thing in hindsight. I jumped into gear and recruited students to promote the show on campus. I remember one special needs girl wanted to wear our painted advertisement box around campus touting the question, "Do the Dead Return?" She had a blast. The auditorium at Fairview filled up that night, and a bunch of folks indicated decisions for Christ.

I was blessed to work with Dennis. He made sure I felt welcomed to this new gig. We enjoyed night skiing at Eldora several times, and I always felt special with him and Barbara. He was bold and organized and fun. I still cherish one of my favorite nick- names from Dennis, "Crooked Hooker." I don't recall the humorous formation of it, but I do know the love and goodwill with which it was bestowed. Nostalgically I refer to Rainey as "Captain, My Captain,"

Months later, in the fall of '73, I was just beginning to feel at home on campus, having talked personally to over two hundred boys that spring. We had a great guy's group working, and I had been joined by Vic Waters from Tampa. When I first started, Principal Frank Hoback had given me a tour of the school and shown me where to meet students. Looking back, it was incredibly liberal of him. I had surveyed and witnessed to guys all over the school that spring—guys in the library, the smoking area, the front yard, backyard, lunch room, courtyard, and gym. The front yard had huge trees shading the grass. Students from Boulder and the nearby University of Colorado would sit and visit and study.

While sharing Christ with a student on the front lawn late one afternoon, it began to sprinkle on us. I had been joined by Dave Beach, a big and spiritually solid eighth grader, who had joined our first Bible study in Boulder. Dave smiled at me inquisitively during the light rain, wondering if we should go inside. This guy was so deep in concentration, he didn't even notice the rain till we finished and he had put his faith in Christ. We had several situations like this where God had prepared people ahead of time and nothing would interfere with their focus on the Good News.

Boulder's high schools were run like universities; the kids might only have four or five scheduled classes of the seven periods and were free to come and go as they pleased. So there were a number of students free each period, just hanging around. Bob Kramer, another student we met on the front lawn, informed me he had already prayed to trust Christ. He had been on the lawn days earlier, listening in on a conversation I was having with another student, and trusted Christ as I read the prayer to the other student. Indeed, he became an integral part of my first guys Bible study along with Jim Holder, a gymnast; Dave Beach, the eighth-grade discus man; Bob Hahn, from choir and drama; Reed Schelke, an all-state pitcher; Greg Stonebreaker; and Mike Smith, a snow skier. Mike was the first student I led to Christ at Boulder. By the next day, when we met for follow-up, he had already shared Christ with his best friend Arnie.

Growing up in South Africa, Mike had come to Boulder to live with his uncle for high school. He had asked for help acquiring his driver's license, and I would let him use my car. One Sunday afternoon we drove up Canyon Road into the mountains from Boulder on a practice run in my stick-shift Camaro. Mike was a smoker and insisted he could drive and smoke at the same time. While flicking the ashes out the front vent window, he lost control, almost taking us off the road! No further instruction was necessary, as the cigarette quickly disappeared out the window!

Beach Evangelism

Mike traveled with my roommate Vic and me to Florida for those conferences at USF. On the day of outreach, we went to the beach to share Christ. We were having fun talking to students on the beach, but it was getting warm, and I decided to wade in while holding our tract up out of the waves. Mike got tickled and joined me. We swam over to a kid on a raft and asked if we could visit. We shared Christ with him and when we finished, he slipped off the raft and knelt in the surf to pray to receive Christ. We didn't notice we had drifted all the way into shore. We went up the beach to meet his folks. I introduced myself and told them about our visit. I recall they were so encouraged about their son's decision. All in all, that summer was so fruitful. Mike headed back to South Africa after our first week in Florida.

Prodigal Bus Trip – A Day of Purpose

Years later Mike returned to Boulder by Greyhound bus for a visit. He had been seated next to a young guy who kept reading the same passage of Scripture over and over. Mike was somewhat out of fellowship himself at the time and this reading and re-reading was driving him crazy. In frustration, he asked the guy if he could help him. The kid gladly accepted.

Seems the seatmate had run away from home numerous times and was returning for one last chance. He had been reading Jesus' story of the prodigal son over and over. Mike immediately understood the Lord's divine seating chart. Saying a quick prayer, he explained the parable and led the fellow passenger to Christ. Upon arriving in Boulder, we had a joyous reunion and rejoiced over his adventure! Now, couldn't the Lord have used a more prepared saint on this duty station?

Mike thought he was just returning to Boulder for a fun reunion with friends. Our sovereign Lord had a higher purpose for this trip and knew he could prod Mike into joining him. Actually, Mike was the perfect choice. He, like the other kid, was a prodigal, but one who knew the Lord and knew his power to reach out beyond the normal etiquette of bus manners to bring someone into his loving kingdom. God's purposes are so much higher than ours, and for that I am grateful.

I had reported for duty in Boulder in January '73 and left in fall '78. It covered parts of six school years. Lots of stories developed during this assignment: battling the ACLU and winning, getting kicked off campus, getting engaged, discipling guys to my first state championship football game, and more.

The Boy Who Got *Really* Saved – A Moment of Intervention

After Dennis Rainey left our Boulder team to become the Great Lakes regional director, I transitioned into his spot at Fairview High for the remainder of my time in Boulder. During our summer projects in Estes Park, I had been reminded that the founder of Cru, Dr. Bright, began at UCLA by reaching leaders on campus. Soon afterwards, I began to pray for and meet key student leaders at school for appointments to discuss their faith. Numerous football and basketball players became involved with us.

One day I had my Bible with me as I visited with guys in the student area. A basketball player started thumbing through my Bible, saying he had been reading his. I teased him to be careful, that he would burn his fingers on my Bible, but all the while loud alarm bells were going off in my head. Not only was this the best basketball player in the school at the time—he was a starter as a sophomore—he was also the toughest guy at Fairview. His fistfights were epic school events that everyone talked about for months. Why anyone would fight him is beyond me.

We had become friends from playing basketball in the rec center, so I asked him if he wanted to visit. He agreed and we slipped into the library and found an empty table. As we worked through the "Four Spiritual Laws" booklet, it was evident God had prepared him. His best friend was a Christian, and so was the girl he dated. Several guys on his Fairview team had become Christ followers.

Not believing what was happening, I asked him if he would like to begin a relationship with God by inviting Christ into his heart. He simply bowed his head and we prayed together. After a brief follow-up explanation of what just happened, we went back into the student area. All of his buddies were still there. As we approached, I asked him to tell them what happened in the library. He said, "You know that thing where you open your heart and invite Christ in? I just did that." You could literally see their jaws drop. A quick survey of who would be most likely to trust Christ at the school would have him near the bottom. He was a loyal friend, very respected and well behaved, just a fierce fighter you didn't want to mess with. And he had just become a Christ follower.

As he began to grow in his faith, he would invite his brothers into his bedroom and read the Bible to them. He became really involved in our Bible studies and conferences. His life changed as he began to trust the Lord, and there were no more fights. He played college basketball on scholarship and married his high school sweetheart. At the thirty-year Cru Boulder banquet, some of his classmates said he and his wife were some of the best parents anyone knew, real role models. Other guys on the team trusted Christ too as a result of his faith.

A counselor at Fairview, who was a fellow believer, told me his daughter had seen us in the library. She didn't know me, but had told him, "Daddy, a boy got really saved today!" I'm not sure what she saw, because our conversation seemed pretty simple and quiet to me, but I know that at another level, there had been a great victory won. I learned later he had chosen to delay an appointment with a famous college coach in order to visit with me. I had no idea the coach was at school that afternoon or that he had put the coach on hold.

On a follow-up note, Tom Chambers moved to Boulder and played basketball at Fairview with him. They made an awesome team. On a bird hunt one afternoon, they encouraged me to try a little dip of tobacco. I had never used dip, nor have I ever used it since! But I figured we were outside and I could spit freely, so in it went. I was cautioned to leave it in for only a few minutes. We reunited sometime later, and they were alarmed that I hadn't spit out the dip. By then, my shotgun had begun to weigh about the same as a cannon from a Spanish galleon. The sky was starting to spin and they made me sit down . . . while they had a good laugh. Chambers went on to play for Seattle and Phoenix in the NBA and was most valuable player at the 1987 NBA All Star Game.

Introduction to Wrestling

While at Fairview, I was introduced to wrestling, which was not a Texas sport in the '60s. A couple of really unique and fun guys, Peter Yee and Bart Woodiel, became involved with Cru from the wrestling team. They taught me how to score matches, which really made watching fun. Bart, who loved wearing overalls without a shirt, wrestled in the 130s, and also played football as a guard. Guard is not a position for 130-pound guys. He would put on a little weight, but I don't think he ever played football at more than 150. His senior year, he practiced so hard and played so well he got promoted to first string. The coach confided to me that he just couldn't keep him off the field. We felt this was a real faith victory. In the state semi-final game, Bart was up against a huge all-state defensive tackle. When the contest was over, this big guy approached Bart with a puzzled look. He couldn't understand how Bart, at his size, had been able to move him around all afternoon. Bart smiled his great smile and gave the Lord the credit.

I recently contacted Bart, who continues to walk with the Lord. Ten years ago he and his wife adopted a brother and sister from an abused and orphaned family of eight children in Columbia. They had lived a tough life in an institution for five years. Bart said the Lord had opened their hearts to love in new ways they had never experienced. He explained how they came to realize in a new and powerful way that our forgiveness and adoption into God's family mirrored their adoption of the Columbian children. The strength and love God gave them to parent these kids has moved Bart to consider starting an orphanage for Columbian children.

The School Board and the ACLU - A Time for Protection

The Boulder Council of Churches had decided they wanted a bigger hand in campus ministry, a heavy hand. They brought a four-point agenda before the school board which included kicking Young Life, FCA, Cru, and other organizations like them off campus; eliminating Christian songs from choir programs; and inviting liberal Council-affiliated churches to teach religion classes on campus. The school board kept tabling the discussion until the churches threatened to hire the ACLU if they didn't get a hearing. This was great, because the school board didn't like being threatened. The president of the board was an incredibly gracious and well-liked woman, Virginia Patterson, who I think was a serious Catholic. A top-notch attorney from my church was also on the board, Ed Hubner. Ed and I met to discuss a strategy.

We decided to work behind the scenes, using phone calls and letters to recruit a nationwide network of prayer. Cru attorneys provided an excellent federal court level brief on the rights of high school students. Ed distributed copies to all of the school board members and their attorney. Anyway, after numerous heated school board meetings with ACLU and Council of Churches members taking the rostrum, the school board, with their attorney's help, drafted their new policy on religion in the schools. Employing wording directly from our legal brief, the board rebuffed the Council of Churches, not bending to any of their demands.

We wound up with a real legal right to be on campus as long as we didn't disrupt the educational process. The only difference was we had to sign in upon arrival each visit. It was a tremendous lesson in spiritual warfare for us. Later that spring, I attended an ACLU meeting on the University of Colorado campus, and they were begging members for funding because they had gone belly-up! After the meeting, I introduced myself to the president, who had represented the churches. He was really nice and pleasant and told me our brief had been excellent. Of course, without the prayer, it probably wouldn't have saved the day. None of our staff took the stand, remaining prayerfully and actively in the background, relying on God, and trusting ourselves to his outcomes.

Kicked Off Campus

One year, maybe spring of '74, I was summoned to the principal's office. We had been trying to get an assembly approved with Christian Olympic wrestlers that would have helped us expand our work. He politely told me that they were backing out of hosting the assembly and that I was no longer welcome to come on campus. This is the same principal who had given me the grand tour a year earlier. Seems the B'nai B'rith attorneys had paid him a visit. He opened a drawer and showed me the beautiful calendar they had given him. I remember thinking to myself how strange it was to get sold down the river for a calendar.

That school year was almost over, so I obliged, meeting with students off campus. The next fall, I sensed a confidence to return campus. The first day I saw the principal, I visited with him in the hallway as if nothing had happened the previous spring. We had access to campus for years afterward.

Overcoming Fear

Leaving campus one afternoon, I got this knot in my gut which convinced me the Lord had wanted me to stay, but I persisted in leaving. A van full of the girls' tennis team was parked next to the side door I exited, ready to leave for a match. They began to sing "Jesus Loves Me" as I snuck by. In my heart, I was figuratively crawling down the sidewalk past them, I so embarrassed. That evening, gaining some perspective and wondering why I let the girls' tennis team shame me, I resolved to handle any similar situations completely differently.

Several months later, as I walked in the front door below the watchful eyes of Jake and Mini, a hippyish student began to mockingly hum "Jesus Loves Me." Fortified with new resolve to not be shamed, I joined arms with him and began to sing out loud as he hummed. My bold theatrics lasted but a few steps as everyone in the front hallway stared and the poor guy slunk away. I boldly marched on with a confident smile on my face, never again afraid on campus.

I began to realize that since God had called me to reach these kids, I actually had more of a right to be on campus than the non-Christian faculty and staff who hadn't been called to work there! Affirmation in relationships and work builds confidence and allows us to humbly go about his work with the expectation of results. Ephesians 2:10 says, "For we are his workmanship, created in Christ Jesus for good works, which God prepared beforehand, that we should walk in them."

This is our confidence that our work and relationships are significant and that we are partnering with him to walk through stuff prepared beforehand. He has already worked out the scenarios; we just participate with faith and love, secure that the outcome is his business!

It continues to be my policy to work behind the scenes through relationships in regard to legal matters. Most educators and coaches know that a Christian student is better academically, behaviorally, and athletically, so they appreciate the work of discipleship we do. We work to become friends with them; they are our peers on campus and return year after year, unlike the kids who do four year stints and exit . . . hopefully! I recently partnered with a vice principal I have known for years to provide a ride to school for a troubled teen, picking him up at the County Juvenile Detention Center. I feel that our partnership with the Lord empowers us to partner with them.

Encouraged by Howard Blandau
– A Weekend of Grace

I'm not sure many people will recognize this name, but this man has a tremendous legacy, especially in my life. Dr. Blandau had been the dean of men at Wheaton during the '60s, when he met Jim Green, the Cru campus director. Cru's emphasis on the Spirit-filled life had a radical impact on the dean. By the time we met him in 1973, he had set up private practice in Philadelphia and become a one- man crusade against legalism in American Christianity.

Dennis Rainey, who trained me in Boulder, had booked Dr. Blandau for a staff retreat. Our board and volunteers joined us in the mountains. We filled out psych profiles and tests ahead of time. Dr. Blandau reviewed the results during individual appointments and taught five lessons on "Freedom in Christ" from Galatians.

The weekend was literally life changing! Our board members were skipping around the room like school kids the last night, free from condemnation and guilt, free in Christ. When you realize and embrace all that Christ's death has freed you from and the promises he has given, it's tough to be sad or boring. It was for freedom that Christ set us free . . . freedom to love and serve others . . . in His power. What an awesome truth. Perhaps because of Howard, I have developed a "legalism meter" of sorts. God is so good and so gracious in his dealings with his children. And that is one truth I want to shout from the rooftops. Our Buckaroo Bible Study has been an experience of grace. Grace has been the underlying theme of all our teachers.

In the Face of Our Ineptitude – A Space for the Goodness of God

The trip back to the airport on my last Brazil mission was horrible: simply, plainly horrible. We developed a good partnership with the Cru staff in Rio De Janiero and made numerous trips with students in the '90s and 2000s. Visiting schools during the day, we saw that God had already built ongoing relationships with teachers, administrators, and kids. We went sightseeing in the afternoons with the Brazilian students and hosted parties at night to share the gospel. I love Brazilians. There is a wonderful naiveté about them. They are as worldly as any European culture, but more childlike. They are quick to make friends and trust others . . . without the jaded American skepticism.

On our last trip, as we prepared to leave the hotel, the staff was instructed to get the Americans onto the bus. But we hit a roadblock on the front steps of the hotel. Fifteen Brazilian students began a time-honored tradition: the "Brazilian Goodbye." I am locked in a front desk shakedown, our hotel wanting $200 US for a missing towel, which probably cost $10. They won't give me our receipt unless we complied. I thought we had cultivated friendships with the management during our two-week stay. Evidently, barhopping that night with our towel money had trumped any friendship we built.

I exited the front doors in no mood for this mob scene of goodbyes. The bus was parked on the curb, and I was shouting at students to get on it. But the Americans were in long sad embraces with the Brazilian kids, looking at me like I didn't exist. We joke about "Brazilian Goodbyes" lasting forever, and it's true.

My plan to make a clean and early getaway to the airport wasn't going to happen. After more un-Christ like yelling and pulling of rank, we were finally ready to leave. One of the most committed Brazilian translators, a kid who showed up night and day to take us places and help, was standing at the door of the bus wanting to ride to the airport with us. I shouted, "NO! No Brazilians on the bus!" and frantically tried to close the bus door. Unfortunately, this door couldn't be closed manually by passengers or angry mission directors. Only the non-English speaking driver behind a closed door could close it. I was shouting, "Cerrado!" which I learned on Sesame Street . . . and which isn't Portuguese but Spanish for "closed."

The kid was begging to come to the airport, he had gifts to distribute to our team and was looking at me like I just shot him in the heart. Our girls were crying. More refusals. I grabbed the gifts from him, hurriedly got the door shut, and we drove away. All the students were crying, none of them sympathetic to their angry over-the-top director, who was the only one concerned with keeping the schedule to the airport. Welcome to leadership, buddy. Sometimes it stinks: sometimes you have to make the tough decisions, like leaving a Brazilian Bambi wounded and dying on some anonymous street just off Catete in Rio de Janeiro.

Thankfully, some miles down the road, the sniffling stopped and I began to hear some quiet talking and muffled laughter. It had been a great trip and I was later able to reconcile online with our gift-bearing translator. You can learn to anticipate spiritual warfare. Attacks are common when least expected. We had our guard up all week, but once the bus arrived, I had relaxed my shield. Still, God is the Lord of broken pieces. His gracious glue puts pieces back together and reinforces the humility that spreads a generous gospel.

After weeks in a foreign country, a well-executed exit is important to me. On these trips, we are trusting God's goodness. His goodness supersedes our lack of spirituality when even our best intentions have gone awry. While he worked in our lives during these trips, I am convinced that his goodness and grace extended equally towards those to whom we were sent. The assurance of his goodness is confirmed from Romans 8:28—that all things work together for good. God is good and, when lifted up, draws all men to himself. It's comforting to trust in a good God whose love and goodness supersede my follies.

The Daddy Hug –
A Moment in His Embrace

In the spring of 2009, we were working in Rio de Janeiro, Brazil, with a group of students from Plano. One of the girls, Lauren, had lost her father at an early age. He had been shot and killed in a drug deal gone bad. In preparing for the trip, I told Lauren that if she was ever homesick or scared she could have a hug from me. At our house, we call this the "Daddy Hug." I really can't recall much hugging on this trip or any mention of the Daddy Hug once we started visiting the schools each day. We had made friends with students from the Methodist school and hosted them at a party one evening. We had food and games, and taught some country western dance steps. As part of the program, Lauren had tearfully shared her story about growing up without a dad. She explained how, as a Christian, the Lord had become her Father and had begun to fill in the empty places in her heart.

We closed in prayer, giving the Brazilians an opportunity to start a relationship with God. I noticed afterward that one of our favorite Brazilian students was crying. Susie and I had met her years earlier as an eighth grader, and now she was a senior. When asked why she was crying, she said Lauren's story was her story. Her dad was living in the US and she rarely saw him. She had prayed with us that evening, beginning her personal relationship with God as her Father. I stepped around to give her my usual side hug and she rebuked me. Waving her finger at me she said forcefully demanded, "No, Benton! I want the Daddy Hug!" I was tickled and shocked at the same time. Lauren must have explained the hug to her, because I had not and she certainly felt she deserved and needed one. While we hugged, I glanced at Lauren, who was laughing with us through her own tears. It was a special evening. Lauren has returned to Rio a couple times to visit her Brazilian friend; it's a friendship that will last because of the Father's love they share.

Much has been written recently about the "father wounds" many believers struggle through. I don't have all the answers; I just know that he pours out his love in our hearts by the power of his Spirit. Surely this daily flow of God's love can fill some of the rough and broken places in others as it has in Lauren's heart.

Children –
An Age for a Protective God

I just sent my youngest progeny, Susanna, off on a five-hour trek back to college in Arkansas after Christmas break. It's the dead of winter, the thermostat reads twenty-nine degrees in her vehicle . . . and I'm wondering what's going through her mind.

What is this separation anxiety I experience now as a boomer adult when grown children take off for college and careers? Are we really separated and from what?

Perhaps the separation is from children as children. In this human journey, the child slowly disappears. In my work, I work with the same age group, fifteen to nineteen years old, people in the tween years, part adult and part child. I relish this age, knowing just how much to expect, just how much responsibility to give, and just how much fun it is to treat them as adults.

When it comes to my own children, it's tough to see them grow up. You are beginning to see the seemingly endless hours of childbearing, coaching, teaching, and encouraging all come to a conclusion. You transition to praying more than talking. Praying for new friends, new directions, deeper walks with God, and against accusations and condemnations of the Devil. This closed-mouth parenthood is the toughest. Your life is still speaking volumes, your walk inspected and dissected, and your love and affection for your wife is foundational. But now, it's text messages of encouragement, emails full of love, and fun updates that are some of your best weapons. Powerful weapons in the arsenal of parental influence.

During breakfast after my weekly men's Bible study, one friend asked about giving advice to his grown child. I suggested, "Only give advice when they ask for it, and even then, be brief! Especially if you want to keep the relationship warm." Several of the guys loved this and keep quoting me. And the Lord has honored it, according to subsequent reports!

Oh, the parental influence goes on and on, yet now it's sometimes a bare-knuckled fight of faith. Daily intervening against a tireless enemy whose stated purpose is the antithesis of your own. Believing God in hope against hope for best outcomes, for the greatest good and happiness of your little children, who have grown up and left you haplessly alone in the home you built with them in mind. And now, when they do return, they sleep in past midday and stay out till all hours with friends in places you never heard of in your own city! You catch only glimpses of them when they pause to eat or check in on social media. Yet we are appreciative and always encouraged when they stay up to visit. We laughingly say that if your grown-up kids call to visit without asking for money, you have succeeded as parents!

Why do we hover and care? Because God cares as the Father, whose protective over-watch is without anxiety. We are motivated by his love and the understanding that trials build faith. And that is where children go: on up the God over-watched faith chain to adulthood and their own responsibilities, handled in their own ways. God bless us one and all!

The Divine View on Self-Pity – A Space for Our Generous God

During high school in Ft. Worth, I learned how to throw a pity party. The first five games of JV football at Paschal High were fun; I was penciled in as a starter in the defensive back-field. We played Grand Prairie the fifth game. Their team kept running around my end in a big power sweep. As the evening progressed, I became a little reluctant to continue to sacrifice my body and my head, which was beginning to spin. The coach began to switch me around to the other side of the defense so my counterpart could have some of the fun. By the next game, I had disappeared from the depth chart and was languishing on the bench . . . in a world of self-pity, far away from the coach and the team. When the coach yelled for me to go in during the second half of the next game, my teammates came running to find me. Buried deep in a miry swamp of self-pity at the end of the bench, I hadn't heard my name being called.

Working now with athletes who are constantly under scrutiny, being moved up and down the roster, forgotten, remembered, appreciated, and yelled at, I have developed some counsel which I hope helps them.

Sulking doesn't help! It suits up and tries to substitute for faith but performs poorly. Some years back, one of our junior guys won the starting role as point guard on the varsity basketball team. He deserved it. The next fall, he fell out of favor with the coach, became the butt of all the coach's derision and scorn, and lost his starting position. I would watch him after practice his senior year in the nearby city rec center. He played with grown men who really had game and ate them alive. Taking out all his frustration on them, he drove the lane unintimidated, playing like a man possessed. He had the skills, but in practice the coach's constant haranguing had paralyzed him.

We prayed through it, but nothing changed that year. Years later, after college, the Lord moved him to confront the coach, who had transferred to a nearby district. He arrived all prayed up. When he entered the gym, the coach stopped practice and called the entire team around to meet him. The coach went on and on to his new players about what an incredible person Kevin was and how he wished he had a son like him, etc. He even called his wife on the spot and told her to put on steaks; he was bringing Kevin home for dinner!

As Kevin recounted the story to me later, he said the coach was oblivious to the way he had hurt him years earlier. So he was able to release him and the years of hurt and anger and move on, past the self-pity. Now Kevin Flannery pastors a church in New England.

I regularly tell the guys not to feel sorry for themselves and ask if they know who is coming to their pity party. Nobody! Satan throws it for you and leaves early, and Jesus never shows up! Feeling sad when hurt by others is healthy. But throwing a pity party because God didn't meet our expectations is deadly. I love what one of the sophomore players, Collin Lee, said about a game this fall when he made a mistake and was taken out. He stood right next to the coach and yelled and cheered for his teammates. The coach put him back in because he was cheering and not sulking, or maybe because he was tired of listening to his cheering. Either way, I love Collin's response.

Beyond Self-Pity –
A Season for His Faithfulness

Over Easter we travelled to Louisiana for a wedding. Flying back, we sat next to a woman who had no time for self-pity. She was a Katrina Ninth Ward survivor and a mother of two. She works in Texas now, where she had eventually relocated. She was flying home from a wedding when we met, and she had a story. When their neighborhood flooded, she and her mom gathered up her two children and began hiking out. With the rising water up to her chest, she put her three-year-old on her shoulders and held her eight-month-old in her arms. As they looked across her neighborhood, they could see the level of the water in the distance was ten feet higher than where they stood. She told me she wasn't making this up. It was as though the Lord held back the water so people could escape.

They approached an evacuation site, where a helicopter

landed right in front of them. Her mom got on, but as she and the children stepped forward, several men bum-rushed the chopper and it took off with her mom on it. She had no idea where her mom was headed, and she was left behind by herself with the two children. She had heard that the Superdome was a tough scene, and she figured she would never survive there with the small children. So she began camping out in the bushes in front of a Walmart, where relief workers were feeding people. She said they had food, but at night there were gunshots and people yelling from cars on the street behind the bushes. It was so scary she couldn't sleep. On the seventh night, worn completely out and not knowing the future, she cried out to the Lord that she couldn't make it another day. Immediately she heard a voice in her soul, "Yes, you can! I didn't bring you this far to leave you now!" Her faith was strengthened, and within two days she was miraculously reunited with her mom in Texas.

I told her about a boy I am working with from the Ninth Ward and asked for her insight. She said the best thing FEMA did for her wasn't food, it was counseling for her children. She said the Ninth Ward was tough, but it still was their world. They felt connected to victims of crimes there and, strangely, to the perpetrators too. The situation was so unique that it's difficult for others to understand. It's hard to relate to what it's like being violently torn out of your home and relocated to somewhere with a different culture, to being called names and shunned as an outcast. She said her oldest boy still has a chip on his shoulder to some degree but that the counseling was helping. She gave me hope for the student I know.

Years later she had been hired by a brokerage firm. During training she overheard another trainee mention he didn't believe in God. She waited till it was break time and approached him, cheerfully inquiring about what he had said. She began to tell her story, and the conversation about Christ changed his whole outlook.

As she asked about what I did, I explained our work, how we were developing future leaders like her—people who weren't ashamed of the gospel and would speak up compassionately and lovingly for Christ. A big smile came across her face as the Lord confirmed her through our visit. I told her the Lord had helped her become a survivor—that it was obvious to all who know her. He didn't bring her that far to leave her now. And the same is true for us because he promises, "I will never leave your nor ever forsake you" (Heb. 13:5).

Observing Trees –
A Time for Gardening

It doesn't take many years living in North Texas to develop an appreciation for trees. After years in this house, we have all of five and a half trees. Sounds silly to those with scads of trees, I know. We have had a couple trees come and go. Some trees, like the oaks, last longer. I have become a fan of the live oak in Texas . . . especially the ones that grow into big umbrella shapes. The Hill Country of Texas is covered with these . . . trimmed up by the nibbling of deer, cattle, and goats. We have one, so I can attest to the fact that live oaks are stately, green all year, and beautiful in their ruggedness.

Many years ago, while walking on the bike path, I once noticed a giant live oak near the Schimelpfenig Library, with five strong branches. At the time, I sensed each branch represented a staff member on our five-person team. The Lord encouraged me that this was the way he saw our team: all connected to the same trunk that was him and all strong because of that connection. I was puzzled, being acutely aware of our weaknesses, and yet I gladly embraced the Lord's perspective of our team. We are sometimes too aware of our own weaknesses and those of our workmates. It's easy to wonder how God would ever get anything done through us, because we feel so inadequate. And this is exactly where God steps in with us, whispering, "When you are weak, I am strong." Our success depends so much more on God's willingness to use weak and broken people to spread his Good News than on any strengths or gifts we bring to the equation. Someone said that simply showing up is half the battle.

I have seen high school kids accept several not-so-cool staff simply because the kids felt safe, cared for, and loved. Kids see right to your heart. They can tell quickly if you care about them. And if they sense that you care, it's not important to them what you look like. It is his love that wins the lost and changes the world.

Speaking of coolness, I have often prayed, "Lord help me look foolish and silly as to better communicate your love." When kids see we are not afraid to make fun of ourselves, it has a calming effect. They think, *Oh! Maybe I don't have to worry so much about being cool.* I am not talking about skits where you dress up like Steve Urkel, with black-rimmed glasses and your pants hiked halfway up your chest. I am saying I really want to look goofy for a purpose. Self-deprecation is a valuable tool for the youth worker.

And so there were the five strong branches, drawing their nourishment from the trunk and anchored in the tree's root system. Jesus explains the importance of our faith connection with him clearly in John 15, during the upper room discourse with his disciples the night before the crucifixion: "I am the vine; you are the branches. Whoever abides in me and I in him, he it is that bears much fruit, for apart from me you can do nothing . . ." (John 15:5).

And so we find ourselves abiding, clinging, adhering to Christ, drawing on his power for the tasks at hand. And we also rest in him, knowing the results of our work are in his hands.

Under the Fig Tree,
a Space for His Sovereignty

Jesus called Nathaniel out from under the fig tree, out from his personal devotions, his private time of prayer. On September 9, 2009, we had freshman chapel at one of the schools. Much goes into this—permissions, securement of drinks, visiting, talk prep, etc. Having invited a youth pastor friend to help, I was caught off guard when he brought a coworker . . . caught off guard spiritually, that is. Satan used a quick shot of jealousy—"the presumptuous pride of home turf" to knock me off-kilter. It was like I was the king of all this domain, and how dare he bring someone without my foreknowledge and consent! Soon I said something I should not have, something I now regret. I was totally out of line, out of character, and it stung the intended person, whose countenance changed the rest of the afternoon.

I felt a quick tug toward God during chapel and fired off short arrow prayers to get back in the Spirit. Upon leaving, I was overwhelmed with remorse. I quickly fought this off, recapturing my faith and wondering how I flipped so quickly. God affirmed my repentance and renewed unity with his Spirit later that day, using me in good visits with friends and a key pastor.

And yet I had to ask forgiveness of my friend, which I did humbly. And perhaps the Lord can restore our depth of friendship, though he sees me plainly now for who I can be at my worst moments.

We also have a fig tree in our yard, under which I, like Nathaniel, devote time to the Lord. "Can anything good come out of Nazareth?" Nathaniel asked. Yes, it can. The Son of David has emerged and is changing my cynical tongue and thoughts. And thank you, Lord, for looking past my stuff and seeing me as you did Nathaniel, a man without guile.

Our generous fig tree, (upper left).

Friendships across the Book – A Season for Mercy

Ever since growing up in Jewish neighborhoods of south Ft. Worth, I have enjoyed the company of Jewish friends. My next door neighbors were the Schwartzbergs. Some of my childhood friends were Lon Werner, Mike Resnikoff, and Mike Tobor; my first girlfriend was Nonie Sonkin. I love the way they phrase things, the way they answer questions with questions, and the confidence with which they talk.

Visiting with an Israeli sailor in the Newark Airport, I asked him why the Jews have moved away from the personal relationship with God that you see with David and Moses. His reply was simple, "It was the Holocaust." The European Jews felt deserted by any personal God after that and have held on to the traditions without the source. The source? Didn't Michener or someone write a book like this? I love these conversations. His dad ran the power supply for Haifa and he was on military leave, touring the states. I shared my faith briefly, yet encouragingly. If you trust Jesus as Messiah for your forgiveness, you are still a Jew. Nothing changes that. You simply become a Jew with a Messiah, yet the costs for this free option were astronomical.

One of my friends went to work for a law firm in Dallas, which was mostly Jewish guys. He said they are very sensitive to Christian/Jewish issues. My dad's best friend for years was a Jewish attorney in Ft. Worth. At lunch one day, he shared his concerns about driving through one of the Ft. Worth suburbs, saying they were very anti-Semitic and he didn't feel safe. I had never heard anything like that and recalled running track meets there and all the countless trips through that area. It became obvious that you can be totally oblivious to prejudice, and I mean totally, if you're not one of the offended party. These Jewish friends were on my teams and in my classes. I played at their homes and loved their families. I knew they were unique, but in my small world, we all worshipped in different places, so it made us more the same than different.

I will be forever grateful and somewhat tickled that one of the things God used to turn me around in college was Mike Tobor. He came to my apartment to borrow a book and took a long look at me, when I was then deep into my hippie stage. "What ever happened to you? You're a bum!" he exclaimed. Mike hadn't seen me since my clean-cut preppy days in high school. And yes, I was a bum, or at least was approaching appearing like one, and this brief visit began to turn me around. I remember smiling foolishly, saying goodbye, and strangely, not being offended. I was going to church every week. This was the only way I knew to touch base with God, though I sensed his presence and conviction often enough. So it's encouraging to think that he loved me enough to use a Jewish friend to hold up a mirror so I could really see who I had become. That spring of my senior year at Texas was the bottom. Within weeks I would join a band of strong Christian guys for work in California . . . and a turning point from which I would never return.

In Psalms 139:1-6, David, another Hebrew amigo, spells out our reality:

"O Lord, you have searched me and known me! You know when I sit down and when I rise up; you discern my thoughts from afar. You search out my path and my lying down and are acquainted with all my ways. Even before a word is on my tongue, behold, O Lord, you know it altogether. You hem me in, behind and before, and lay your hand upon me. Such knowledge is too wonderful for me; it is high; I cannot attain it."

Thank you, Mike; thank you, merciful Lord! Thank you that you gave me only so much rope, that you kept close and pulled me out into your presence with these good men.

Adventures in Adult Courage – A Day Requiring His Protection

There are things in life over which you exercise no control. One prime example is whom God provides as siblings. My brothers, Randy and Phil, have been a great blessing to me. Phil and his wife purchased a lake house, which made me sad only because it is 2.5 hours away; I've always wished it were closer! I loved it there, with its beautiful vistas over Possum Kingdom Lake. It was a great home which hosted several great family gatherings.

One cold weekend, Phil and I ventured out fully clothed on his Sea-Doos®. Like motorcycles on bumpy water, they hit 35 mph pretty quick, which I wasn't ready for psychologically. Phil kept racing away from me till I got up my nerve. Hitting the waves at 35 mph is real man stuff. We chased ducks and looked at homes as we headed all the way across the lake and

The Hall Family:
Phil, Benton Jr., Me, Mom, and Randy.

up the Brazos River.

So, where did this courage come from? It came incrementally, from 10 mph, up to 20 mph, then 25 and 30. Courage starts with small steps of faith, then more faith, as our vision of God becomes larger and larger. So it progresses in the Spirit, from things like riding Sea-Doos® to doing the hard and right things at work and in relationships.

The Lord coaxes us out into the deep waters of adventure just as he did when he called Peter out of the boat in the midst of the storm. He knew Peter could do it, and Peter did take a few steps. The key to water walking seems to be in keeping our eyes on Jesus. When Peter lost eye contact and looked at the wind and waves, he began to sink. It gives me a sense of security when Jesus saves him and gets him back in the boat, calming the storm.

He used a natural event to pump up his disciples' faith, but he wouldn't let Peter drown. It's scary when we swim into the deep end of the pool, but we have the assurance that he knows

the depth and is with us. In the dark of the storm, Jesus identified himself to his men like this, "Take courage! It is I!" (Matt.
14:27). And so it is two thousand years later: we are called to
take the courage he offers to do live life with him, whether we
find ourselves splashing playfully in the shallow end or tread-
ing water in the deep end. He loves us, we can trust him; he's
got this.

God's Place in Life and Death – A Time for Sovereignty

Each June for over thirty years, Cru has trekked students to the Y Camp in Rocky Mountain National Park, northwest of Denver. The Y, at 7,500 feet above sea level, is within the park and sports an incredible view in all directions. We run a discipleship conference complete with nationally known speakers and live praise. We sandwich the input and discipleship training between tons of fun activities. One summer brought a dark stranger into the mix . . . death. Several of our kids and staff witnessed the gruesome death of a girl from a Michigan youth group unattached to the RMGA.

At the back of the main Estes Park municipal parking lot is a beautiful park, replete with trees, grass, a stream, and a fifty-foot rock wall. Several of our buses had brought students into Estes Park for shopping that day. A little before departure time, some boys from our camp got up on top of the wall. Large rocks were loosened, tumbling down upon Audra Brownell, taking her life. This quick, shocking death happened within ten feet of several of our staff and students and bus driver.

What impact does that have on a student? It depends on what they witnessed, how old they are, how mature they are, and what personality they have. It's tough to measure the impact of witnessing an event like this. For some, what they witnessed is suppressed, as is the case with one of our staff. She knows she saw it happen, but God has graciously suppressed the images. Over time, I think, these vivid memories, overseen by a sovereign and loving God, are released when he knows we can handle them.

God empowers students to work through these experiences taking proper perspective and responsibility. Our conference was impacted specifically as our kids saw the reality of life and the certainty of death snatching it away. Within days of the accident, six hundred kids were dispersed on vans, buses, and cars into surrounding communities on a scheduled outreach to share the hope of Christ. The students had a super-charged passion and compassion for others. Over one thousand conversations later, they returned victorious to share all that transpired. The loving power of the Holy Spirit was released through bold conversations, challenging untested assumptions and selfish worldviews. We could not help but notice the palpable rejoicing and release, which was certainly absent earlier in the week.

The reality of life and death should motivate us all to walk closer to the Lord by faith, embracing the commandments to love him and love others, and the great commission to make disciples of all nations. I don't see how these propositions can be separated; the commitment to discipleship should flow naturally from the love he pours out in our hearts by his Spirit. Wouldn't we want to bring others in on this incredible adventure of faith, hope, and love?

Block Party, Beer, and Hugs, a Night of God's Love

When Susie and I moved into this neighborhood twenty-odd years ago, there were families with young children, and several of them hosted block parties. Everyone brought something to eat, and we all had a really good time. Then, Rod, the neighborhood party guy, moved to another city, and kids like mine grew up. Sadly, a childless silence ensued. Recently, a newer neighbor hosted a garage party. He came bounding over onto my front porch, so excited and happy, and wouldn't leave till I had assured him we would indeed come to his party.

As he left, I came back in to explain to Susie, who having overheard the conversation, said, "We should be the ones hosting the party." Music to my ears! Yes, we *should* be. It's funny, but throwing parties every week in the form of Bible studies and outreaches for kids seems to sap any desire to host neighborhood parties. Most nights when not out at a game or study, we sit home enjoying each other's company, alone.

But that night we toddled through the rain a couple doors down, entered a home we had never been in, met people we did not know, and had a really great time.

Alert for the leading of the Spirit, I found myself affirming the life of a neighbor a few years older. We pulled fun and great stories out of him and wound up speaking some encouragement into his life.

Later a baseball-capped gal with a large satchel slung across one shoulder poked her head around the corner. Shortly after meeting her, she blurted out to everyone that she and her housemate had not felt safe in every neighborhood, but they did in ours. I assumed she had enjoyed some of the contents of her satchel once I discovered it was full of her favorite brand of brew. Within minutes of brief conversation, she was hugging me around the shoulders, only to be followed by more hugs an hour or so later between snatches of talk.

I think she saw Christ in me. She kept saying, "You're a great guy." Emphasis on *great*, like she was surprised. It made me think, in the midst of one of these sweet hugs, how much the Lord wanted to hug her and draw her to himself.

Good friend Barry Woods wrote a book on destiny and destiny moments. These are those instances when you know the Lord has prepared the way for you in conversations and circumstances so that you can represent him. The neighborhood party was one of those days. Ha! My most fun days are laced with incidents of his leading and empowering with his desire to encourage someone.

I am a big "hug person." Even before the party, I was with a friend at the Y and gave him a hug. Earlier at breakfast, I hugged another friend, so twelve hours later, a sweet neighbor was hugging me. Our host hugged my wife as we left the party. Interestingly, no one seemed to have problems getting into conversations that night. Everyone wanted to talk. Shy ones, loud ones, older ones, confused ones, sober ones, wet ones, little ones . . . all willing to visit and glad for the chance. Not one found himself in front of the TV. There was background music, but it was white noise. For an hour I actually sat in a ninety-five degree garage with a fan blowing on me, talking with neighbors. The conversations were well lubricated, for sure, but they came pouring out. Some were private, some were funny, some were informational, but all were warm, friendly, and powerful. Then there were the hugs. Maybe America needs more neighborhood parties. I am sure we need more hugs.

Rolling with Change – A Time with His Spirit

During the economic downtown, Susie and I were saddened at the news that our YMCA was closing. It wasn't just a workout facility; it had been a social hub for my wife and some of her closest friends for over ten years. The facility had been owned and operated by EDS for their employees. It was situated in beautiful trees above a well-maintained creek, surrounded by soccer and athletic fields. It contained an indoor pool, an elevated track, and all the necessary classrooms, childcare, offices, gym, weights, cardio machines, etc. There was a deli, a full-time massage therapist, and a chiropractor. Tons of people used it, and it was a genuinely fun place to work out.

At the same time the economy slid, Life Time Fitness wedged itself into the market, just down the street. Life Time offered an outdoor pool and newer, cooler amenities. There was a loud sucking sound as our Y members flocked to the newer, hipper Life Time.

Is anything ever supposed to remain the same? Don't we all leave homes, change cities, make new friends, change jobs, start families, and take on new responsibilities?

Doesn't the Lord expect us to change, too, under his direction and empowerment? In 2 Corinthians 5, he reminds us: "old things have passed away, behold, new things have come."

So I will try to enjoy and appreciate any blessings the Lord sends my way, whether material or spiritual. I will faithfully steward, knowing that he owns these blessings and responsibilities and entrusts them to me for a time and a purpose. From the parables of the ruler leaving servants in charge of different amounts of money, I know not everyone gets the same responsibilities. My responsibilities may change from time to time, according to his direction. So I am embracing the change at the Y with the appropriate amount of sadness and shooing the melancholy moments away that lead to anger. Boy, how I enjoyed that old YMCA!

Men and Women Who Sacrifice
– An Era of Purpose

This morning I find myself seated on comfortable outdoor furniture on a Tuscan-ish patio overlooking a fountain-fed pool, surrounded by natural Texas landscaping and live oaks. In the back of the yard stands an Austin Chalk wall shielding us from the road. We are in Austin with friends Travis and Loretta Lowe to watch our nephew, Nate Boyer, play in the UT vs. Wyoming game. After five years of service, he had left Army Special Forces at twenty-nine to go to college. He chose Texas and tried out the football team as a walk-on, having never played. Coach Brown kept him, and after a couple years, they gave him three one-year scholarships as the deep snapper. Nate's dad Steve is with us on this trip along with our daughter, Susanna. The stage is set for some first-class fun.

Nate, #37, is scheduled to carry the American flag into the

Nephew Nate Boyer, former Green Beret, running the flag for the Texas Longhorns and deployed in Middle East

game along with Samuel Oacho manning the Texas flag. This game was carried on ESPN, and friends from all over the country texted Nate . . . it was incredible. He told us afterward that the hardest part was trying to see through the fog Texas shoots out from the tunnel into the end zone for dramatic effect. All he could see were his feet as he tried not to run into the goalpost!

In the locker room, after Texas won the game, he was surprised to receive the game ball from Coach Mack Brown. Asked to give a speech, Nate, sensitive to his position as a rookie, was reluctant to say anything. But when they insisted, he told them that when the Special Forces was his team, one of their standing values was "We fight for the man on our left and we fight for the man on our right." He equated this to his new teammates at Texas fighting for each other. When his dad recounted this story to us at dinner the next night, he teared up. It brought tears to all of us, especially in light of the life and death situations Nate experienced on the field of combat.

Most guys realize there are more important things at stake in life, like war, no matter how important and exciting your current gig. Yet the knowledge that people have sacrificed to ensure our freedom allows us to appreciate and enjoy life even more. For the Christian, Christ's sacrifice gives us purpose. Colossians 3:24-25 encourages us that work is service to him: "Whatever you do, work heartily, as for the Lord and not for men, knowing that from the Lord you will receive the inheritance as your reward. You are serving the Lord Christ."

And so, whatever we do, work or recreation or service, we engage heartily for the Lord, knowing we serve him, assured of our purpose and its significance because we belong to him.

Coaching in Small Town Texas – Two Years of the Father's Love

This fall our nephew, Nate, got us tickets to his Longhorn game against UCLA in Jerry Jones's AT&T Stadium. We landed on the fourteenth row, the 45 yard line, in wonderful padded seats, so much nicer than the family section in Austin. I struck up a conversation with the big guy next to me. He had coached one of the defensive linemen who would become a first round draft pick after his junior year at Texas. He told me his son and the lineman played together and had become good friends. When things had gotten tough for the Texas player, the coach's family took him in for a couple years at their home. After sharing about our work with students, I discovered the coach and his wife were Christians and how their faith fueled their love for this kid. They helped him get baptized while he was staying with them and encouraged his spiritual journey.

Years later, he was still making sure the coach had tickets to some of his games.

Texas led most of the way, but UCLA scored at the very end to win the game. Family members trundled underneath the stadium to wait for the players to exit the locker room. This huge lineman emerged head down, face saddened. I was standing nearby when the big coach asked what was wrong. The lineman dejectedly mumbled, "We lost." What happened next caught me off guard, and I get choked up each time I relate this story. In a flash, the middle-aged coach reached over railing that separated them and enveloped the huge player in his arms. Man to man, father to adopted son, I heard him whisper, "Come here, sweetheart." I quickly withdrew, sensing that to continue to listen would have been intruding in something almost sacred.

Please don't be put off by our Texas lingo, and you will have to trust me on this: it was sincere. It wasn't a power play or done for show. It happened so fast, it had to have been done numerous times in a loving home. What's the big picture? The Lord's fatherly love is awesome and instantaneous. He has enlisted average, everyday, humble people to spread it around. They are changing the world, one hug at a time, two years at a time.

"This Thing We Do" . . . Living by Faith and Not by Sight – A Juncture of Faithfulness

This past week, I found myself visiting at a number of Thursday night football games. Like a Sanguine tornado, I made contacts with parents, kids, and administrators. Going deep in some conversations, shallow in others, I saw the Lord push our student work way down the road. Fifteen minutes after a brief conversation with the Plano quarterback from twenty years ago, Tom Radtke, I was approached by his freshman cheerleader daughter. "Hello, Mr. Hall, I'm Jordan and I will be joining your club!" The next week, she was introduced to another member of our staff, Nicole Matuska, and helped arrange a coffee outing with several friends, two of whom trusted Christ. Not every game yields results like this, but the

Lord usually makes something good happen.

I recently fielded a call from our headquarters to discuss the significance of this thing we do called Cru High School. I traded stories with my immediate report, Lee Cooksey, about the lasting effects of our work and the current status of friends and family. Perhaps heaven is for eternity, because it will take that long to thank everyone who played some part in our spiritual growth. And only then will we fully grasp the significance and scope of all that we have trusted God for in this life. For now, it is enough that we live by faith and not by sight, believing that "This Thing We Do" is the thing he led us into, empowering us to accomplish for the glory of his Son.

Special Students –
A Season of Blessings

There have been a number of special students who served as leaders in our work, and I wanted to tell the stories of a couple of them, Chris Howard and Rex Burkhead. Both these guys were already on track for something special when they joined Cru, and we rejoice in the ways the Lord is using them years later.

Chris Howard wore a tie to school all through high school. Joining Cru along with many of his friends, he already stood out. While at Plano, he led off-season Bible studies for us with football players. He became student body president, head of Jr. ROTC, and captain and starting running back on the 1986 State Championship football team. Chris played at the Air Force Academy, became a Rhodes Scholar, rose to the rank of lieutenant colonel in the Air Force Reserves, and will be the next president of Robert Morris University in Pittsburgh. When he returned to speak at one of our student leadership breakfasts, I presented Chris a picture of him leading a Bible study his senior year. He was wearing his classic white shirt and tie.

Rex Burkhead influenced an entire city by his faith and character. He graduated seven years ago and people still talk about him. He humbly made friendships across the social and moral spectrum, and you couldn't help but like him. His work ethic and running style made us all cheer for him. Like Chris Howard, he played running back for Plano on really good teams . . . teams made better because of Rex. He played for Nebraska and is now in his third year with the Bengals, playing alongside quarterback Andy Dalton, another Cru leader from Katy, Texas. Rex served as a Cru leader, participating in skits, leading small groups at conferences, and opening a thousand doors for Cru. How many times I dropped his name for the sake of expanding the kingdom is an unknown, but it's ever increasing. He married Danielle Wiggans, who hosted our leadership meetings in her home.

It's impossible to estimate the influence guys like Chris and Rex have on football- crazy towns like Plano. They were friendly and approachable. Their humility served as a multiplier to the public impact of their faith. They have been loved and appreciated by so many families and students.

The Rally at Clark Stadium and Death by Heroin – A Moment for a Protective God

In the late '90s Plano made national news when fifteen young people died of heroin overdoses over a two-year period. Mexican brown tar heroin was being distributed in pill form at parties as "Chiva." Labeling and packaging were key. Kids weren't tying off arms and sticking heroin-filled syringes into themselves. They were swallowing pills of something they equated to speed or ecstasy with warm, thrilling effect, blissfully ignorant that Chiva was Mexican slang for heroin. Something as good as this at $10 a pill spread quickly throughout the youth culture across all ethnic and socioeconomic levels. Sadly, so did the deaths by overdose.

Alarms were sounded and the public became aware. There

were numerous organized citywide meetings and public forums. Solutions came from the public sectors; the police, schools, and city government all responded quickly. In one of these meetings, Father David Roseberry of Christ Church stepped to the microphone and suggested the city officials had not considered the possibility of help from local churches. Most of these city leaders were churchgoers themselves, and this became a fairly good sized "Aha!" moment. A Pastors Task Force was formed as a representative coalition of local pastors addressing the heroin problem. Over a series of meetings, the churches developed plans to help, including a citywide youth event.

Several local church youth pastors and parachurch guys had been operating as "The Pack" since 1985. Cru had been involved since its inception, and by default of age and experience, I had become its de facto head. By the late '90s we had developed an incredibly broad reach from traditional Protestant denominations to Catholic, Assemblies of God, Pentecostal, Bible Church, and Church of Christ guys. Anyone understanding Christianity in North Texas will realize only God could have pulled this off. We really cared about and respected one another. The Pack had developed far more unity across the city than the head pastors did. We approached the Pastors Task Force and suggested we be the ones to pull off a citywide youth rally. They readily agreed, so the "Rally at Clark Stadium" came into being.

We solicited fundraising help from Cindy Kuykendall, who energetically drug me around the city, raising about $30,000 for the production. The Lord went before us, as we were able to obtain use of Clark Stadium, which traditionally had been reserved for school events only. The stadium is named after John Clark, former Plano football coach and Texas coaching legend. In the '70s Coach Clark had worked with Cowboys head coach Tom Landry to establish Fellowship of Christian Athletes in Plano. We are still friends to this day, and his faith has cast a long Christ-honoring shadow on our city. It was only appropriate that we would present Christ as the answer in a stadium named after this incredible, humble gentleman. Securing the funding and the stadium were confirmation to the Pack that God was in this venture.

While at TCU, I had been involved in student government as head of the entertainment committee, whose job was concert and event promotion. Amazing how the Lord positions you for future work he has prepared beforehand. Thirty years after promoting Neil Diamond at TCU, I took the lead with tremendous help from several savvy youth guys, like Jim Williams at Prairie Creek. Youth guys promoted the rally in their churches and secured volunteer help for setup, take down, security, ticket sales, etc. Cindy publicized the event so well, most of the major networks pushed out remote news teams for coverage on local affiliates.

We had no feel for what would transpire; we just wanted Christ to be lifted up through the concert and speaker. By the evening of the event, I was toast. Jim was running the floor and all systems were go. Thousands of kids began to show up, and we were off and running. After the concert, I found myself lying down on the 20 yard line in the dark, just soaking up the moment. Nearby, I could hear the CBS affiliate reporter during his live report. He was talking about what an incredible evening it had been. Joy erupted in my heart: we had done it! Even the secular press felt it was a success. The unity of the body of Christ, working together with the city, had been used of God to accomplish his purposes. Hundreds come to Christ that night and were followed up in their friends' churches. The drug traffickers were arrested and tried in federal courts and sentenced without parole, and our protective God answered thousands of prayers to stem the scourge of heroin use and the deaths that followed. There were three rallies, each unique and a story unto themselves. I am privileged the Lord gave me a role to serve in these Christ-honoring events, because my faith was never the same.

The Artistic Layman –
A Season with a Creative God

Long ago and far away, I discovered I appreciated art. Perhaps it was haunting the Amon Carter Museum of Western Art during college or dates to Casa Mañana musicals. It could have even been the feeling that my clothes didn't work in high school. But sometime in my twenties and thirties, I acknowledged that I loved art. My mom got an art degree from Our Lady of the Lake in San Antonio, and we enjoy visiting the Ft. Worth art museums. My longtime amigo, Chuck Wallace, is an artist and has developed his hobby into something which Susie and I love. We have framed several of his watercolors and hope to acquire more. Chuck takes classes and enters competitions to sharpen his skill. Yet art takes several shapes and forms beyond the easel, and in some of those I have become a dabbler of sorts!

This weekend, partly because of art, I removed the last of our blackberry bushes. Our home and yard are my easels: a setting for my creative juices, requiring me, like Adam, tossed from the garden of Eden, to toil among thorns, weeds, and fire ants to create something beautiful.

Our hopeful blackberry experiment in fresh backyard fruit was a qualified bust. Importing vines from my wife's home in Oregon and planting them along our picket fence provided us with rats and rabbits and mockingbirds, but no luscious berries. Before any of the tiny fruits could ripen, they were ransacked and plundered in the vicious circle of North Texas critter life.

Manned with rake, lopping shears, and electric hedge trimmer, I went to work on this failed and overgrown agronomy project. Seems the thorny blackberry bush itself loved North Texas soil while refusing to issue forth the same succulent fruit the sandy soils of Oregon produce. After several sweaty, laborious hours, accompanied by cutting and bloodletting reminiscent of the prophets of Baal on Mt. Carmel, the task neared completion.

I called in reinforcements from the "high school guy pickup truck world" to aid in recycling this vegetative waste. Andrew arrived with his recently inherited Chevy truck, complete with sprayed-on bed liner. We made a couple trips to the dump, during which I informed him he had a decision to make. Was this going to be a guy truck or a girl truck, to which he calmly and immediately answered, "Oh, most definitely, both!" He intends to haul things and do manly chores in it while keeping it spotless and pristine for the ladies. Good luck, Andrew!

As I acknowledge my artistic leanings, I ask, isn't every child an artist? Don't they all love to paint and mold and crayon and color? Isn't this proof of our connection to the cre-

*Landscaped backyard and picket fence with the bike path
and utility easement just beyond.*

ative Creator God of the Universe, who has painted millions
of sunrises and sunsets, fashioned colorful tropical fish, and
designed billions of people so that none of us are the same? I
believe we glorify him when we create, re-create, and acces-
sorize yards, cars, clothing, homes, work places, etc. Doesn't
he love to stir these creative juices and glory in our design and
fabric and landscape?

He is in the business of crafting us in the image of his Son,
pulling out all the inner beauty that was gifted to us. And as
we cooperate by faith and faithfully align with his purposes,
we reflect his glory joyfully. He won't leave you alone to your
own purposes. He gently and constantly serves up his glorious
plans and designs for you to sign off on and submit to. And
he delights in the beauty of his Bride, all of us doing our part
in the power of the Holy Spirit. Sometimes we hear the faint
notes of this discordant symphony of believers, but to him it is
melodious and grand. Yes, it could always be better, and as we
strive for humble unity, its sounds reach further and further

into dark places, spreading the hope and peace and love of Christ.

So budding artists all, do not think lightly upon your gifts and talents; whether you're a musician, artist, actor, mechanic, draftsman, or athlete, press on for the higher call. For these creative endeavors align us with our Creator who loves abundantly and can't wait to see what you bring him next!

*The Call for Privacy - A Time for the Simplicity of Christ

I sent my kids a picture of the fence this morning, cleared of all vines, and received a reply from one of our children about my removal of the last vestige of privacy. Our house is now open to the world . . . not the bedroom/bathroom section, but the living area, where we spend most of our time. Kitchen, dining room, and den areas all combine into one nice large room facing north, with our yard rolling out onto a miles long bike path and utility easement. Our last house was a collection of dark chopped-up rooms, so we designed an opened and windowed house. No fewer than eight windows and a glass door grace the north side of this space, rendering views of our yard and a bordering picket fence. The curtains on these windows are open always, unless it's twenty degrees and blowing outside. And since this is North Texas, well, you get the picture . . . and so can anyone else walking, running, or skating by.

And thus the modest comments elicited from our kids have found their context. Openness works both ways, we argue, since we love the view. This would never have worked for my father, however, who from time to time considered our entire Ft. Worth home his naked room; his confidence was buoyed by a house full of boys and curtained/shuttered windows.

The Buckaroo Bible Study – An Epoch of God's Faithfulness

The Buckaroo Bible Study is a thirty-year "Work in Progress." Good friend and fraternity pledge brother Rob Farrell had been organizing Cowboy Gatherings in West Texas for a couple years when some guys trusted Christ at Cowboy Church on a Sunday morning. Cowboy Church is the first event on Sundays, the final day—no church, no breakfast. So 90 percent of the guys attend. Dudley Hall is our perennial speaker for these events, which also include music. Rob started the Buckaroo Study on Friday mornings to help the guys who had decided for Christ learn more about their new faith. He asked Dudley to teach. We thought it would be a six-week event. God had another idea. Over the years, tons of guys have filtered in and out, with usually twenty to thirty in attendance. Dudley is still our main teacher, but Barry Wood subs in when

Dudley can't make it, and I sub when neither of them are in town. After the study, most of us pile into Corner Bakery for breakfast and fellowship.

Some of the Buckaroos have become involved with excellent ministries. I like to think that the faith atmosphere created in the group has had something to do with it. Bob Stevenson is a "Holy Smoker" at Prince of Peace Lutheran. They raise funds at Easter, selling smoked turkeys and hams. The proceeds pay for hotdogs and hamburgers at events like our Cru Volleyball outreach. This fall, eight students trusted Christ when the "Smokers" helped, and we share the joy with them!

Another man spearheads a ministry for heroin addicts; another started a camp after his son died where kids with disabilities come for a week. Heart patients attend one week, diabetes patients another, cancer patients another, and kids with muscular dystrophy another week. Dan Bailey has started "Just Say Yes," a national speakers forum that focuses on making right choices and abstinence. Another started a ministry in New Orleans in an apartment complex . . . crime there is now near zero. Many serve on boards of charities, and all support various churches and para-church organizations. It's an eclectic group of guys from different churches and occupations. We have a lot of fun, and there have been some very humorous moments along with a ton of answered prayers, longtime fellowships, and lifelong friendships. Several of the Buckaroos pray for me each week when they get my texts and emails. I always follow up with photos of the events they prayed for. There are some regionally well-known people in the group and some unknown, all are good men, surrendering to his work in their lives at some level.

Over the years of teaching, I would guess grace has been our consistent theme. We covered it today from a new angle, and it runs deep in our psyche. I would readily admit that my theology has been most grown by Dudley Hall's teaching. He is so real and vulnerable and, I think, brilliant. Dudley approaches a passage or topic and takes us closer to God in our faith walk, emphasizing faith and God's availability. Whether teaching from the Old Testament or the New, his work always points us to Christ. One of my favorite series was from the book of John on the Fatherhood of God. This series became the book *Orphans No More*. My favorite is his classic *Grace Works,* which he republished in 2015. His ministry is called Kerygma Ventures, and there are a ton of great resources on his website.

Dudley is a consummate bird hunter and usually has a couple of well-heeled bird dogs. On a spring turkey hunt along the Brazos, I peppered him with questions, which he patiently answered. We kept hearing one turkey in the distance and would occasionally scratch our turkey call box trying to lure it over. We never saw anything. Wrapping up the hunt, we realized the other two guys thought they were onto a tom also. Checking coordinates, it appears we were calling each other. Dud claims to this day that I fell asleep in the sun on a big rock. Not wanting to substantiate any scurrilous accusations, I will just say it was a refreshing time in the woods and, as usual, I learned a lot from my time with Dud.

Some time ago, an old friend in trouble called Dudley, needing $13,000. Dudley corralled the money and sent it to him. Years later the same guy wrote Dud's ministry a check for $1,300,000, which he used to begin work on the Tesoro Escondido conference center on the Brazos River. Ben and I have attended a father/son retreat there. Hundreds have attended pastors' conferences, father/daughter gatherings, and leadership conferences there. It's a great faith story which continues to this day.

Barry Woods, our first substitute teacher, is one of my he-

The Buckaroo Bible Study: Rob Farrell, Josh Huffman (major donor to Tales), Tom Goodson, Bryan Sutherlin, and Jerry Green.

roes. He is seventy-nine years old. He came to Christ in high school and became a traveling evangelist. Wherever you travel with him in Texas, he claims to have preached revivals somewhere nearby. And for these claims, he receives a good deal of teasing. I brought students to a meeting at Rosemont Junior High in Ft. Worth where he spoke to a full house of high school kids in 1972. He pastored a church in Hollywood and one in Lubbock before he left the ministry for several years. After a stint in commercial real estate, the Lord recommissioned him to ministry. His key men are Africans who take the gospel all over Kenya, Tanzania, and several other countries. They have a tremendous impact, sharing Christ with millions each year, using the Jesus film and starting churches as part of the follow-up. I told him I want to be like him when I grow up! The author of *Destiny: You and God*, a book I really enjoy, Barry was also a baseball player. Now he loves hunting and has become a patient golfing partner of mine along with a couple other Buckaroos.

Our group has migrated around Preston Center from office buildings to bank cellars to restaurants to our current location at Gold's Gym. Wherever we land, the Lord seems to show up and encourage the men. The singing starts at 7 a.m., led by Bill Heard. We end with prayer and head over to Corner Bakery for breakfast. Sammy Davis has kept a watchful eye on us for over ten years there, reserving our table and serving our chow. We have become good friends, and a couple of us attended his mom's funeral in Oak Cliff. One thing the men have developed is a sweet love and concern for each other. We rejoice with those who rejoice, and we weep with those who weep. It is my privilege to know these men. I have been truly blessed.

Reflections on Alignment and Compliance – A Time for Patience

Fall 2013 had been both fruitful and humbling. Called into a principal's office, I found myself humbly receiving the news that I was being brought into compliance with district policy on religion in the school. As I sat there listening to what amounted to a kindly executed verbal beat-down by a friend, I pondered my options. I had none. Regaling this administrator with the glorious history and results of my work in this district was not going to help me in any way. I felt led by the Lord to merely sit on my thumbs and take it silently, which I did.

The coach who accompanied me also sat quietly until asked if we had any questions. At this point he inquired if this new edict also meant that we could no longer distribute candy canes at Christmastime. (He was referencing a nationally publicized lawsuit against our district for the rights of students to distribute candy canes to school friends)

This perfectly timed, humorous comment relieved most of the tension that had accrued up to this point. As the principal laughed with us, he said, "No, we can distribute candy canes and we can actually call it Christmas again!"

Afterwards, I began to tell friends that compliance was the Word of the Month for me. So I am coming into compliance. God is still in charge! We can still facilitate the work; it will just have to be student initiated and run.

As kind as the principal was (and he is an ally), I still came away feeling gut punched, so I drifted into Country Burger to drown my sorrows in a tall glass of my favorite mixed drink: A&W Root Beer and Diet Dr. Pepper. The Lord graciously positioned Ralph Hinds, Jason McNeely, and Marshall Jackson inside Country Burger that day for my benefit. All three graduated in the '80s and were involved with us. It served as further confirmation that God is in all of this.

As funny stories spilled out for almost an hour, these guys really encouraged me. When I left, Jason told me he had been listening to a guest on 90.9 KCBI radio the other day on fear and doubt. He had been fearful about his son, Jason Jr., heading off to college. Junior was one of our Cru leaders.

Jason Sr. said it was like the Lord reached into his truck and shook him during the radio program, saying, "Jason Jr.'s college is *my* job! Stop worrying! I am going to take care of that!" My work in Cru Dallas is his work. I am going to keep it that way and not worry about it!

A Time of Opportunity

"What do you want me to do for you?"
—Jesus to the blind men of Jericho (Mark 10:51)

It's Thanksgiving, and I am thanking the Lord for early birthday celebrations with family and gifts from kids: Apple TV and a Dallas Museum of Art membership. I'm grateful for the awesome soup and birthday cake from Susie and for Saturday date night at Blue Mesa, one of our favorite Mexican restaurants.

Reflecting on all the pieces of Cru Dallas work on the horizon (conferences, a mission to Spain, the golf fundraiser, oversight travel, and weekly ministry), I'm trying to keep them within the bounds of his grace. I put together a mailing piece for Thanksgiving, highlighting all the things we are for which we are truly thankful. I also sent specialized emails to several friends and donors as a November funding ask. Some of them, who texted in the past, "Let's touch base tomorrow," or "I'll call you later today," haven't followed through. These promised callbacks never came. So I sincerely find myself asking again, "Lord, have I done this same thing to others?"

While trying to keep all this in the context of grace, yet owning my own stuff and executing the responsibility of it, I pray, "Father reveal to me where I have not kept promises to others, that my faithfulness would glorify you." God is ministering to me this week as I am moving through the Psalms and some Philippians studies with Don Anderson's devotional, *A Great While before Day*. Also encouraged by Dudley's Buckaroo teaching on grace, I am realizing that our purpose in confessing sins is so we can be with God, not just modify our behavior or feel absolved . . . though I certainly revel in my absolution from the penalty of sin, thankfully!

The question becomes, "Do I really want to be with God or do I just want His stuff . . . guidance, power, funding, protection?" I'm sensing some hesitation early this morning as I wrestled with this while still in bed, hot and hurting with back pain and confused. Do I want to go back to sleep? Or do I want to get up with God? Sometimes, I am afraid of what he might say to me. And if I am not listening, I am afraid I could miss some of his will . . . which might just be that I should *listen*! There is no extra charge for these brilliant moments of insight. Ha! It's just Basic Christianity 102.

Wasn't I just recently wrestling with his question, "What do you want me to do for you?" It's the question Jesus asks the blind Bartimaeus on the way out of Jericho for the last time. And the same question he asks another blind man as he enters Jericho. There's something eye-opening about these blind guys and Zaccheus seeing clearly who Jesus was as Messiah, Son of David, when the religious leaders could not.

I had spent weeks mulling the Jesus question over, knowing he was asking, "What do you want me to do for you, Benton?" And I knew it was about more than just my top-forty prayer request list. I had decided that my answer was "I wanted to walk in all the good works that he prepared beforehand for me to walk in" (Eph. 2:10), completing the tasks he assigned to me from before the beginning of time. First and foremost of these tasks must and needs to be walking with him. Being with him. Delighting myself in him. Knowing that he delights in me and returning his love. As we like to say in the Buckaroo Bible Study, "I'm with him!" Please spread the word when anyone discovers a better place to be!

Reaching into Unsuspecting Corners of Granada – A Week of His Grace

One of our distinctive attributes is taking students overseas, helping them share their faith in new contexts. We go by request of staff in those countries and by permission of the principals in the schools.

What can you say about a trip to Spain with awesome students and staff and lots of prayer backing? Olé! What a magnificent trip the Lord orchestrated! We were able to engage students at good levels of spiritual interest and as friends. We were so well accepted and cared for, it made us feel special. The kids could not have known how special they were to us. Each game, each class, each small group discussion took them deeper into our hearts. Because it was such a rushed trip, it almost didn't seem real. No sooner had we become used to a routine in Malaga than we bussed our way to Granada. The briefing for our time in Granada was in the monastery where we were staying. You could sense the excitement of Patry and Omar, the Shine staff (Cru High School in Spain). Jen was an American teacher working at St. Augustinos, the private school we would visit. She was hosting us and arranged our busy schedule, which they had printed out for us. It began that night with flamenco dancing and dinner in Centro Granada.

The next morning, after a great breakfast of coffee, breads, and fruit, we hit taxis for a quick trip to school. St. Augustinos is a private Catholic school with great facilities and staff. They ushered us into class after class, where we introduced ourselves and played games with them to improve their fluency in English. After the games, we broke into smaller conversation groups. Our students, having worked classrooms in Malaga, knew the drill and executed flawlessly. As they got to know the students, I took time to visit with the staff, beginning with the assistant director. He was older, but running full speed. We had an engaging conversation, during which I began to discover that he was a brother in Christ. We connected at a deep friendship level quickly.

As the day wore on, we tumbled out onto the school's athletic area and played football, soccer, and volleyball. We also just visited with the students. A group of boys surrounded us, asking questions about life in the US and God. One boy asked earnest questions about God. I shared God's grace and goodness, answering questions about work in a bad economy and the purposes of God for men. A common response from Spanish boys who find they agree with you is a thoughtful, head- nodding, "Yes, *(pause)* I think so." You sense they understand some of the discussion and want to digest it more. If they nod quickly with smiles . . . it's total agreement.

Classroom small group discussion at St. Augustinos.

Within minutes, I found myself visiting with another group of guys. As they introduced themselves, they pointed out a boy and gave him a nickname, one that was not flattering. He smiled sheepishly, stepping back, but not completely out of the group. I smiled, not accepting their name. I asked his real name, not allowing them to brand one of the others as the runt of the group. Jesus would never go for that classification system, and it naturally bothered me. I worked to dignify the boy, graciously introducing myself and purposely engaging him. (By his grace, I have worked these conversations in numerous contexts. I want these "left out" guys to know the love of Christ . . . like Jesus did, pulling Zaccheus out of the sycamore tree. I want to pull them out of racism and every other kind of exclusion into his wide arms of grace.)

The last day at St. Augustinos, I got into a conversation with the director. At thirty-eight, he is brilliant, engaging, fun, and constantly moving all over his school. He whisked me into his office, which he rarely used. So fun to learn that he too knows the grace of God. He had instructed our staff in Granada that the Americans should talk to their students about Jesus, Jesus, Jesus! He showed me a huge book of church documents over the course of history, including some of the writings of Martin Luther. I asked why they would have Luther's writings in a Catholic book. He proudly announced, "Luther was Augustinian!" Ha! Remembering that conversation, I am now laughing hard from deep within. I love these God moments. Who can determine the depth of these? Only God can guide us into the depth of *them*.

Jack Daniels, a Dodge Hemi, and the Big Man – A Night of Powerful Forgiveness

One recent spring I returned home at night from a football banquet, surprised to find a huge black Dodge Ram Hemi parked in my driveway. A big man stood leaning against the tailgate. I was on the phone with a player from the banquet. Explaining the circumstances, I said, "Morris, call the cops if you don't hear back from me in fifteen minutes!"

My first concern was for Susie, who was easily viewable from the front porch as she watched TV. Had this big hulking guy been to my front door? I hadn't gotten a panicked call from home.

Pulling on my "Texas big-boy pants" and igniting any sleepy faith, I parked at the curb and approached the truck.

Our dialogue follows:

> Me: "Hey, how's it going?"
> Him: "Fine, I'm doing good."
> Me: "Do you know where you are?"
> Him: "Yeah, I'm here at my parents' house."

He was doing really fine, floating on a sea of Jack Daniels. My brain fired up mega zillions of synapse-spewing calculations: his age, based on owning this truck; his size, clothes, and face; neighbors old enough to be his folks . . . working down the street, house after house until—*bingo!*

> Me: "I think your folks live four doors down."
> Him: "Oh, hey, I'm sorry. Let me do you a favor, buddy, and move this big rig out of your driveway."

Empowered by his politeness and sensing a God moment developing, I interrupted, playing off his desire to do me a favor.

> Me: "Just a minute, big man, let me do you a favor . . . Do you know Jesus?"
> Him: "I do! I do know the good Lord Jesus!" he cried, sobbing.

And, with a big *boom*, the Lord launched a forty-five minute divine intervention, as my newfound friend now refers to it, punctuated with tears and hugs. This big man was indeed a big MAN, having served our country in Mogadishu, Iraq, and Afghanistan as part of the US Special Forces. Nine of his men had died in his arms. Each had asked the same question, "Why do I have to die over here?" Each heard the same answer as he held them and patted them into their next lives. "The good Lord Jesus has you now."

He had driven twelve hours from the Midwest to check on his folks after an ice storm. He got into Dallas after the storm and grabbed dinner with an army buddy, whose brother was one of the nine. They had found their way through the bottle of Jack. I sensed a heavy sadness and resignation in his slurred speech. At one point, after one of his hugs, he offered to start another bottle with me. I declined but am honored to be considered worthy of such fellowship with this American patriot and warrior.

Soldiers are asked to do terrible things in battle that could bury the average believer in doubt and fear and condemnation. He said they did some nasty "stuff" (expletive deleted) over there that he wasn't sure God could forgive. I encouraged him, saying that we paid our soldiers to do that nasty stuff and God's forgiveness and grace was more sufficient than we could ever know. More hugs.

I wanted him to know the truth of what he had shared nine times, that the good Lord Jesus does have us now . . . in his strong arms of never-ending love, forgiveness, and grace. After more hugs, where I literally disappeared in his strong arms, he spoke reluctantly, "I don't like to ask for f-f-fuh, f-f-fuh, favors, but would you watch out for my folks?" I assured him we would keep an eye on his aging parents.

It had been quite an evening. As he somberly (and soberly) climbed into his truck, I said through tears of my own, "Big man, I think you pulled into the right driveway tonight after all." Thankfully, Susie was clueless about what had happened in the driveway and why her husband was all choked up.

And I am grateful and honored that the Lord chose to use me to encourage one of our bravest men. God's heart is always directed toward reconciliation, and I am sure it broke his heart that this soldier was uncertain about our Savior's complete work of forgiveness. We can so easily accept demonic condemnation as the voice of God. Our perceived unworthiness becomes a relentless taskmaster, whipping us into believing more lies and accusations, when the truth is that our sin doesn't catch God by surprise—it grieves him, of course—but it never alters the constant, powerful, life-changing love pouring forth from his Son. How he would love to hug and pat thousands of believing soldiers, servicemen and women, and whisper, "The good Lord Jesus has you now!"

The Long View – A Season of Faithfulness

The Cru Boulder team invited me to return for their thirty-year anniversary banquet. I felt privileged and was so encouraged to see students I had worked with from the '70s. They were married and their kids were involved. It struck me that the success of our work could best be measured by the long view of what they are doing twenty to thirty years down the road.

The short view can be discouraging. I once paid an unannounced visit to James, a former high school tennis player involved in Cru, who was attending a local college. When I came around the corner of his dorm room, I stumbled upon him sitting in a chair, laughing, beer in hand and girl on lap. Thankfully, they were all fully clothed, lights on . . . and very surprised to see me. What do you say: "Hello, young lady, I'm

Benton Hall, James' Bible study leader. He's one of my top students"? These humorous yet sad moments can short circuit your belief in God's power to change lives.

So I have learned to take the long view on youth ministry. What are these guys doing twenty or thirty years down the road, where the Lord has had more time to pull them in?

Shortly after I arrived in Plano, the Lord gathered a group of guys in our sphere of influence who have gone on to make quite an impact for him. Sometimes you step into seasons like this. It doesn't happen every year. This group was so fun and enjoyed good seasons of football as teammates. Three have become pastors, several have worked with Cru, one has worked overseas in Baptist missions for years, one became a youth pastor, and one worked inner-city ethnic ministry and was given the keys to the high school he was influencing. I am including a picture of several of them from one of our golf fundraisers. From the left: Lee Cooksey is currently chief of staff for Cru High School, which means he is my direct report, my boss! Kirk Perrin and Scott Faulkner build homes and disciple men, who in turn disciple other men. Ron Brennan runs his own business and leads a men's Bible study. And there is me, astonished at these men and blessed, blessed, *blessed* to be their friend.

The Long View with Families

Working in a city for thirty-five years allows ample time to be involved with generations of families. Two of our favorites have been the Smiths and the Jacksons. Larry and Judy Jackson became friends soon after we arrived. I pitched Larry on our work at his son's JV football game in Lewisville. He had been involved in Cru's "Here's Life, America" nationwide evangelistic campaign in Plano. We had a great visit, and he and Judy soon joined our advisory board.

We had contacted Larry's son, Marshall, at practice. After we explained Cru, Marshall told us in a tired and exhausted voice that if we were starting up a Bible study, he was in. We suggested he invite guys over to his house for an introductory meeting.

When we pulled into his cul–de–sac several days later, there were cars everywhere. I walked in on thirty-five guys. Judy had fed all of them more than adequately! Marshall had invited the entire JV team over to his house. Ten of these guys became involved in my first Plano small group Bible study.

Years later, Marshall and his wife, Mabrie, hosted our freshman Cru meetings all year when their son James became involved. Cru has been a Jackson family tradition, from father to son to grandson. We honored Judy at one of our banquets for all the help and encouragement they had provided in getting us established in Dallas.

Our first year in Plano, I also met former Plano school board member, C. Dan Smith. He joined our financial support team, and a couple years later I became friends with his adult son Mark. For years they have played in all our golf tournaments. As Mark's son Colby entered high school, we plugged him and his friends into Cru. Colby became one of our leaders, and I performed his wedding this year to Chandler Stewart, whom he met at Cru. As a community movement, we work with a lot of families. I enjoy getting to know parents and their kids. It seems to be just the natural progression of our work, a part I really enjoy.

Borrowing an overused phrase, Jesus is not finished with us yet. If he were, we probably wouldn't be here, so there is hope yet of changed lives by his power. So I adopt the long view on discipleship, knowing I am not the only impact for Christ in their lives, just one of many . . . and he loves them too much to leave them alone!

On the Hot Seat in Cool Montreal – A Day of Protection

Our national field ministry team took a number of future leaders to Canada for some international service and to expand their faith. Cru's "Power to Change" staff in Canada asked us to help them start a teen ministry. In Canada, high school goes to the eleventh grade, essentially. Then they attend schools called CEGEPS for twelfth and thirteenth grades, where students range in age from seventeen to nineteen. These are run just like junior colleges in the US. While there, students prepare for vocational work or prep for university. Universities are three-year schools. We met with Canadian staff of Cru in their downtown offices and along with their staff visited the CEGEPS they had targeted.

While these are run like open colleges, there was also an element of security: grown men in uniform. Our team spread out in the cafeteria of one of the schools and began to visit with Canadian students. I was sitting with Tim Ehrhart at a table off to the edge of the giant room, near one of the doors. While we visited with Canadians, I couldn't help but notice our national director, Darryl Smith, clear across the room. He stood out in his starched bright-blue shirt and tan corduroy jacket. Then I watched the security guy approach him and engage in conversation. I could detect by their body language that the visit began to take on an official nature in the wrong direction. I leaned over to Tim. "Tim, it looks like Darryl is going to be thrown out by that security cop. I have been thrown out of schools before, and it's not happening again today. Let's go!" Tim and I laughed as we slipped out the back door unnoticed into the underground connection with a huge shopping mall. We shared Christ with college students from the school in the food court area till Darryl and the rest of the team showed up. Darryl has teased me several times since then, because he did get asked to leave campus. When security heard they were with an American Christian group, his demeanor changed and they were given the not-so-friendly heave-ho.

The Canadian staff went right back to the same school the next day, undeterred, and have since begun a national outreach to the CEGEPS as a result of our visit. I get emails from Daniel, their CEGEPS staff leader, who is growing the work on several campuses. Obviously the Lord protected them in starting up this work, so if bumbling, brightly adorned Americans were any help at all, then all the glory goes to God!

A Word about Friendships – A Time for Fellowship

Over the years I have been blessed with good friends. Youth ministry has its unique challenges, so those who have experienced it have a common bond. Such it is with me and guys in this picture. For years we served in Cru High School, in both Dallas and Houston. Like a band of brothers, we have worked tons of student events and staff conferences together. Our history is rich with stories.

For years, the four of us secured apartments together in Ft. Collins, Colorado, at Cru staff conferences. Our children grew up together attending our student conferences. The wives sat up late nights in the hallways of camp dorms visiting while babies fell asleep. Years and years of serving together has built some of the richest fellowship I could hope to experience.

After we served in the Cru Minneapolis training center,

Steve Cooper and I scouted out Dallas area schools in 1979 to restart Cru. We lined up a visit with John Clark, the athletic director in Plano. Our team had been visiting with pastors, school officials, and businessmen all over Dallas. Coach Clark had won two state championships in his ten years coaching Plano and had personally brought FCA to Plano. We knew we were walking into a really important appointment that day. Steve had played on a state championship team in Odessa and later at TCU. Coach asked him several questions about his coaches and his playing days. We could tell he was enjoying our visit. We explained what we had done in other schools to help students find Christ and that we were trying to decide where to land. Near the end of a great visit, Coach said, "Well, I sure hope the Lord leads you guys to come to Plano." Coop and I shook his hand and thanked him for his generous time. Once outside, we started punching each other and cheering. Coach Clark's response was the first real clear direction we had received anywhere in weeks of appointments, and we both sensed the Lord working. This was John Clark giving us the thumbs-up.

Coach Clark and I became friends in the years that followed. I saw him this fall and said, "Coach, I bet you never guessed I would still be around after all these years." He laughed, saying, "Benton, frankly I never thought I would be around this long!" He had come to Plano from Jacksonville, Texas, and thought he would return after a year or two. I assured him it was never my life plan to spend thirty-five years in Plano; evidently it wasn't his, either! Funny how the Lord works!

Coop left Plano after a couple years to lead our Knoxville, Tennessee, ministry and then transitioned to Houston. He loves the outdoors and started our regional "Men's Farminar" at his family's land outside of Brownwood. For years, all the

Longtime amigos:
Me, Chuck Wallace, Steve Cooper, and Zeke
Zeiler in downtown Ft. Collins, Colorado.

Cru staff guys from the Houston, San Antonio, and Dallas teams would meet up for a long weekend of hunting, eating, and fellowship. Now Steve runs "Waking the Passion," a men's ministry in Houston. Zeke and Chuck transferred to Bridges, Cru's outreach to foreign exchange students. We continue our annual couples' retreats and pray through each other's stuff. I once heard a men's speaker say that men needed the fellowship of other men. We have needs our wives cannot meet, and though they might try to help us, these needs can only be met in the fellowship of other men. I have been blessed with all the good men God has placed in my life, and I hope I can return the blessings.

Postscript on Friendship

As I wrap up my collection of stories, I have to mention a couple of friends and longtime contributors to our work and this book. Mike Richards was a steer roping friend of several guys in our Friday morning Buckaroo Bible Study and joined the group years ago. He is a longtime fixture in Dallas real estate, currently hanging his shingle at Republic Title. Mike had a ranch in Bosque County, south of Ft. Worth. My son Ben and I have hunted this ranch several times, and I took a couple of trigger-happy students varmint hunting there.

After lunch at the ranch one weekend, I was solicited by my hosts, Mike and his wife, Fiona, to share a story around the table. I read one about lessons learned from our dog, Hunter. Their positive response was a real turning point for me. I had been reluctant to move ahead with publishing the stories, and without Mike's faithful nudges over the years, *Tales* may never have hit the presses.

In the summer of 1967, Rob Farrell and I pledged the same fraternity at Texas Christian University. We became good friends, and I called him when I returned to Texas with Cru after a seven-year absence. Right away he asked me to teach a couples' Bible study. This Tuesday night group lasted for four or five years, providing us with great memories and lasting friendships. There are many good Rob Farrell stories, and they are his to share. I was blessed to have figured into one of them when he found Christ as a result of our Bible study. He and his wife Holly have opened their hearts to us and our work.

Rob loves playing tricks. Late one night, during a Cru campout on his ranch, an entire tent full of girls quickly scrambled out into the darkness when they heard a rattlesnake just behind their tent. Now I am not saying this was Rob's doing, but on another trip, some boys were excited to find a frozen rattlesnake in their gear. There have been a ton of great memories made on his ranch, and I'm sure there are more to come!

One evening, as I was preparing to teach the Buckaroo Bible Study, I sensed the Lord encouraging me to share a couple of the unpublished stories. The next morning I got the same impression, so I found two that went along with the lesson. At the end of the study, I shared the stories. It got really quiet, which I took as a good sign. At our post-study Corner Bakery breakfast, Rob and Mike pulled me aside and said I should publish these stories as a book. They offered to help make it happen, and they have. We have agreed that all proceeds will go into the Cru Dallas Scholarship Fund to help students attend our discipleship conferences.

Rob and Mike and their families have funded a ton of ministry, both stateside and abroad. Their hearts are toward the Lord, and I am privileged to be their friend. I dedicate these stories to them. Thanks, men. I love you guys.